A journey to a better you awaits you...

This book belongs to

....

....

BLUEROSE PUBLISHERS
India | U.K.

Copyright © Barkha Nayak 2024

All rights reserved by author. No part of this publication may be reproduced, stored in a retrieval system or transmitted in any form or by any means, electronic, mechanical, photocopying, recording or otherwise, without the prior permission of the author. Although every precaution has been taken to verify the accuracy of the information contained herein, the publisher assume no responsibility for any errors or omissions. No liability is assumed for damages that may result from the use of information contained within.

BlueRose Publishers takes no responsibility for any damages, losses, or liabilities that may arise from the use or misuse of the information, products, or services provided in this publication.

For permissions requests or inquiries regarding this publication,
please contact:

BLUEROSE PUBLISHERS
www.BlueRoseONE.com
info@bluerosepublishers.com
+91 8882 898 898
+4407342408967

ISBN: 978-93-341-3735-4

First Edition: October 2024

Mental Health A-Z

Because life doesn't come with a manual!

Barkha Nayak

Welcome to your safe space!

Let's make your mental health journey a little lighter, one page at a time.

Note from Author

Hello, you lovely human!

If you're reading this, you've already taken the first step towards personal transformation and THAT is awesome! Take a pause and appreciate the effort. It matters!

As for me, I've spent 12 years working as a therapist, and trainer to help people navigate the messy business of being human. As a psychologist trained in RECBT at AEI, New York, I'm all about using evidence-based techniques that actually work. Over the years, clients have told me how the creative and structured methods we used in therapy helped them create their own 'manuals' & 'guides' for life—like a personalized toolkit to navigate their mental health.

This Action-Packed Guided Workbook is a result of this fantastic feedback, plus, me chasing my ADHD impulse! Whether you're one of my clients or someone I am yet to meet, I wanted to create something affordable & practical for you. This insightful Self-Help Guide is my passion project. Think of it as a quirky therapist (me), on your shelf, helping you in your mental health journey!

I'm truly honoured that you chose me!

Together, we'll make sure you're on the path to be Better (and Sparklier) YOU!

Warmly,
Barkha Nayak
Founder, Manahsparsh

manahsparsh.therapy

Gratitude

For the first time ever, I want to thank myself! While self-appreciation isn't easy for me, I deserve it for pushing through countless ideas and imperfections to make this self-help guide a reality. It's been a journey of growth, and I'm proud of the resilience and focus that got me here.

Compiling the content for this workbook wouldn't have been possible without the knowledge accumulated over years of education, experience, countless books, hundreds of clients, and the thousands of unseen sources that have shaped my understanding.

To my incredible team—Simantika Chanchani and Kunjal Purohit—thank you for your sharp eyes and invaluable attention to detail. I deeply appreciate the time and effort you dedicated to editing this project.

A special shoutout to Atomoxetine for keeping me focused and helping me tackle perfectionism, one task at a time. This workbook is dedicated to the many humans, like myself, navigating the complexities of life. To my clients and everyone who has inspired my work—thank you for trusting me with your journey.

Why Mental Health A-Z?

Because Life Doesn't Come with a Manual.
Mental health is complex, but it doesn't have to be overwhelming. That's where this Personalized Mental Health Toolkit comes in, designed for the clarity you've always wanted, but with an extra touch of fun!

What's Inside?

Mix of Formats: This is not your typical, repetitive journal. It's an Action-Packed Guided Workbook, offering a variety of exercises: customizable action plans, guided worksheets, quizzes, visual activities, thought-provoking questions, and creative prompts to help you mark, write, and color your way to self-discovery.

Your Mental Health, Simplified: The goal is to help you understand, reflect, discover, and set goals. Track every aspect of your mental well-being with clear, actionable steps.

What Makes This Journal Different?

User-Friendly: Simple, structured, and beautifully designed. Whether digital or printed, it's easy to navigate, reusable, and flexible to fit your unique journey.

Insightful & Research-Backed: Every section is thoughtfully crafted, and is evidence-based, ensuring you get reliable and applicable information to understand your mental health better. No fluff, just real-life, relatable tools for real change.

What IT's NOT?

It's not boring or unnecessarily time-consuming.
It's not another generic journal filled with internet advice.
It's not like anything else you've used before!

How to use?

Think of this workbook like your favorite playlist—no need to follow a set order! Skip to any section that resonates with what you're feeling right now. Work through it in a calm headspace so when things get tough, you can revisit it and rely on its guidance

Here's How to Get the Most Out of It:

- ✓ **Go at your own pace:** Find a rhythm that fits your life and energy—there's no rush. Whether you use it daily, weekly, or only when things get tough, this workbook is always here for you.

- ✓ **No strict routine required:** Not into consistency? No worries! Start slow, pause, pick it up when you need it—there's no rush. This guide will be just as useful now as it will be 10, 20, or even 50 years from now.

- ✓ **Revisit as needed:** Each module offers reliable information and insightful exercises you can return to again and again. Revisiting helps you apply what you've learned, while repeating them helps track your personal growth over time.

DISCLAIMER:

While this workbook is crafted by psychologists using proven therapy techniques, it is not a substitute for professional therapy, medication, or medical advice. Mental health is not one-size-fits-all. If this workbook doesn't work for you, or triggers distress, please seek professional help immediately.

Index

Sr. No.	Mental Health Tip A-Z	Exercises	Pg. No.
1	**A:** Accept Yourself	Circle of self | Best have Blemishes	01-04
2	**B:** Be kind to yourself	Replace yourself	05-07
3	**C:** Cultivate meaningful Relationships	Strengthening relationships	08-11
4	**D:** Do things that matter	The PLUS Factor | Activities Menu Card	12-14
5	**E:** Evaluate Long Term	Cost Benefit Analysis	15-16
6	**F:** Focus on Greys	All things Grey | How Grey am I?	17-19
7	**G:** Get Quality Sleep	My Good Night Ritual | Sleep Tracker	20-24
8	**H:** Have realistic Expectations	Expectation vs Outcome | Challenging "shoulds"	25-27
9	**I:** Improve Capacity to Tolerate Shit	Pain is Gain | Endure & Conquer	28-31
10	**J:** Jot Down your strengths	My Superpowers	32-34
11	**K:** Know & tame your stress	Goodbye Stress	35-37
12	**L:** Look at life as a whole	Life's a pie	38-39
13	**M:** Maintain Balanced Lifestyle	Time Detective | Audit your Lifestyle	40-42
14	**N:** Navigate through your emotions	What am I feeling?| Unpacking emotions	43-46
15	**O:** Overcome Fear of Judgement	Me vs What people think	47-49
16	**P:** Practice Self Regulation	Impulse Tracker | Roadmap to self control	50-52
17	**Q:** Question your Thoughts	Sort my thoughts | Fix my thoughts	53-55
18	**R:** Recognize your role in your distress	How I upset myself | How to stop upsetting myself	56-58
19	**S:** Seek help when needed	My Safety Squad | My therapist	59-60
20	**T:** Tackle Procrastination	Decoding procrastination | Get things Done Bingo	61-63
21	**U:** Uncover your patterns	Thought-reaction connection | One situation, Many reactions	64-66
22	**V:** Value what helped you	The contributors | Gratitude Journal	67-69
23	**W:** Work on your Body	Habit Tracker	70-72
24	**X:** eXpress Assertively	My communication styles | Being Assertive	73-76
25	**Y:** Yearn to set & achieve your goals	SMART goals | Goals at a glance	77-81
26	**Z:** Zero down focus on controllable	Break overthinking | Circle of control	82-84

Accept Yourself

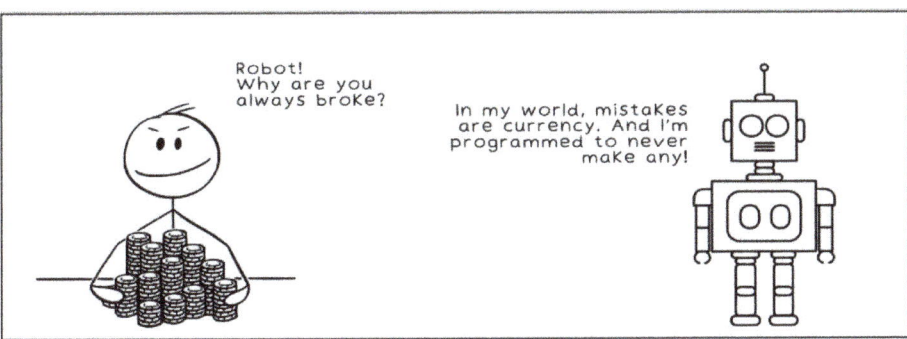

Imagine a world where mistakes are money. How rich would you be?

Unfortunately, in our human world, mistakes aren't currency, and we're not programmed to avoid them like robots. Then, why is it so hard for us to accept our flaws and imperfections? It is because we are conditioned to believe that flaws, mistakes & failures were an anomaly? But aren't they common to all humans!

> Self-acceptance is the ability to acknowledge that you are a complex, imperfect human being, capable of making mistakes as well as significant accomplishments. It is the understanding that just like EVERYONE ELSE you are also a deeply fallible human!

What are the benefits of Self Acceptence?

1. Intact, stable self-image and a strong sense of self.
2. Belief of self not overly affected by external factors.
3. Realistic expectations from self.
4. Greater self-reliance and belief in your abilities.
5. Provides the freedom and flexibility to learn from your experiences and grow.

"Accepting yourself unconditionally, is the most important aspect of growth"

— Albert Ellis

Circle of Self

This exercise is meant to help you see yourself in a balanced, realistic way. In areas marked with a '+', write your positives (things you do well, successes, strengths etc). In areas marked with a '-', write your negatives (things you do badly, failures, weaknesses etc). Consider +ve & -ve aspects of thoughts, emotions, habits, experiences, outcomes, relationships, characteristics that you have!

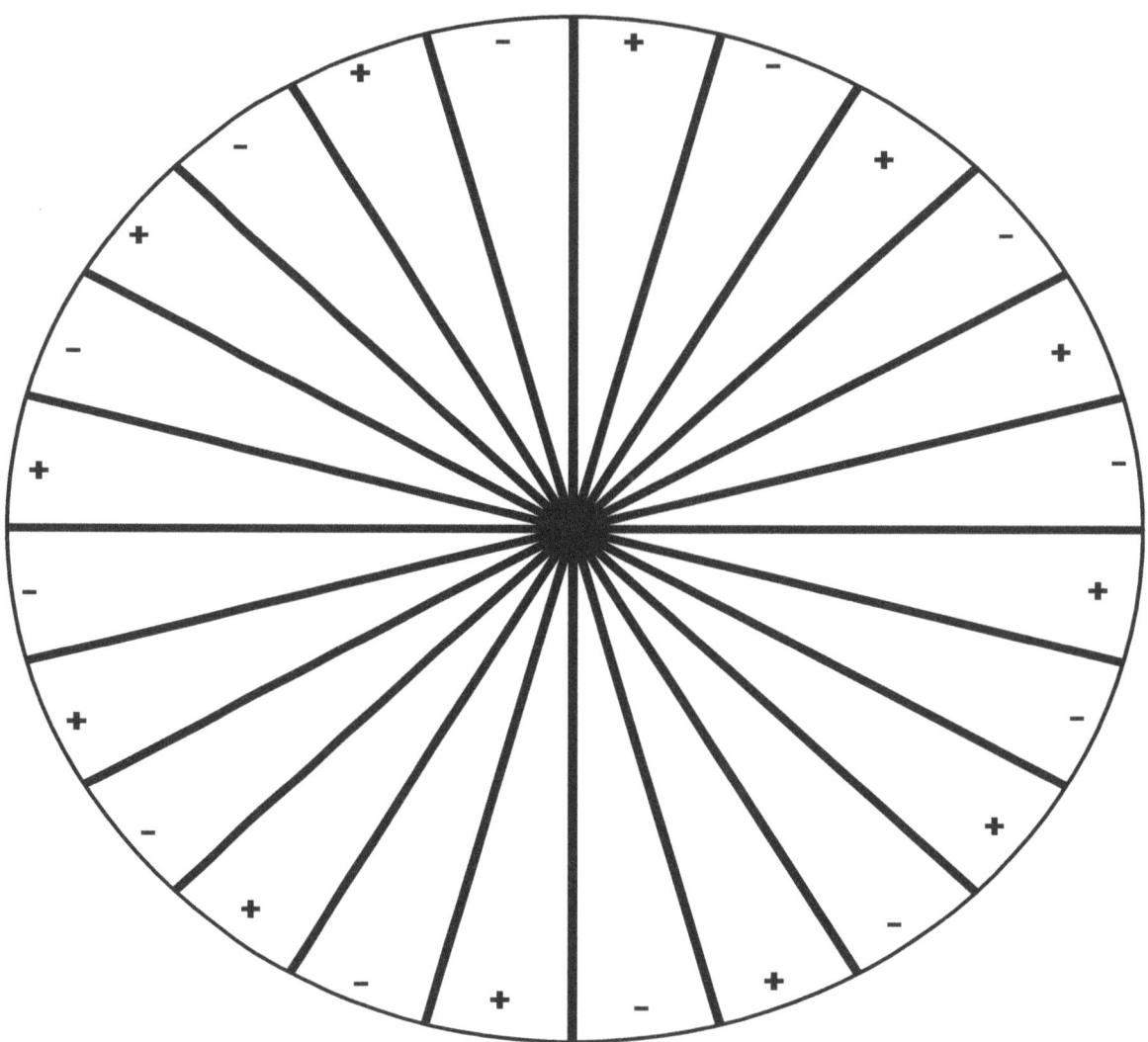

Notice how your circle is a mix of both positives and negatives. No amount of negatives can take away from the existing positives just like positives cannot subtract the negatives. No one can ever be entirely good or bad. Embrace this as a symbol of being a human with the potential for both success and growth.

The Best have Blemishes

Embrace self-acceptance by recognizing that even those you admire have flaws & failures. List people you admire in 1st column & note their flaws, failures, or mistakes in the next column.

Imperfections are universal! If they can have shortcoming, so can you!

Those I admire	Negatives
J.K Rowling	Rejected for publishing for 6 years
Avengers	Failed to stop Thanos
Ranveer Singh, Lady Gaga	Ridiculed for their clothing
Oprah, Steve Jobs, Walt Disney	Fired because of mistakes they made

I've missed more than 9000 shots in my career. I've lost almost 300 games. 26 times, I've been trusted to take the game winning shot and missed. I've failed over and over and over again in my life. And that is why I succeed.

- Michael Jordon

Do these Practical Experiments

1. Ask 5 people around you if they have ever made a mistake, and recognize that it is possible.

2. Request your doctor to write you a prescription for "anti-mistake" supplements.

3. Go to a hospital and get yourself a vaccine against failure.

4. Go to a pharmacy and get an over the counter "flaw-control" pill.

Affirmations for accepting yourself

| "I am not a robot! I am not programmed for perfection" | "Just like all other humans, I am FLAW-SOME!" | "I by default can make mistakes" | "I am a perfectly imperfect human!" |

Be Kind to Yourself

Relatable? Why is it so easy to be kind to others, but not to ourselves?

Kindness towards oneself starts with self-acceptance. It means offering yourself the same compassion and respect that you'd give to a loved one. Think of it like being your own best friend—would you ever harshly criticize your best friend for a slip-up? No? Then why do it to yourself?

Now, imagine working for a boss who constantly puts you down but praises a colleague for the exact same idea. Or a teacher who gives you zero points while your classmate gets full marks for the same answer. You'd hate it, right? It's unfair and hurtful. Stop being that unfair and harsh boss to yourself.

> *"Talk to yourself like you would to someone you love."*
>
> – Brené Brown

What happens when you are kind to yourself...

Helps you recover from setbacks and keeps you motivated

Promotes a healthier relationship with oneself

Strengthens motivation and belief in abilities

Reduces emotional distress

Guide to be Kind to Yourself

Do's

- Empathy & understanding towards circumstances
- Forgiveness
- Respectful self talk
- Judging actions & outcomes but not self "I failed but I am not a failure"
- Flexible & realistic
- Encourage to keep trying
  Faith and belief in abilities, potential

Dont's

- Too harsh and critical towards self irrespective of circumstances
- Blaming, punishing yourself
- Insulting or deprecating self talk
- Labelling yourself "worthless" "loser" "failure"
- No room for mistakes & failures
- Discourage, demotivate
- Self doubt in abilities and potential

Affirmations

"My actions and outcomes cannot define me."

"I am not other people's opinions & judgments"

"My worth does not depend on anything. I am valuable as long as I am HUMAN"

"I have the capacity and potential to change & improve"

💡 Tips

1. Address yourself by your name and talk to yourself in 3rd person. E.g. instead of "I am not good enough" try saying "Barkha is not good enough" The distancing gives perspective immediately, making self criticism easy to check!

2. Think of yourself as cold, hard cash—your value doesn't depend on market trends. You're not Bitcoin; you're a crisp 100-rupee note, always valuable.

Replace yourself

List down recent experiences and note down the self-critical thoughts you had. Then, rewrite those thoughts as if you were speaking to a loved one. Reflect on how this changes your perspective.

Situation	What I thought or said to myself	What would I tell a loved one in the exact same situation?
E.g: Made a stupid mistake during the presentation	I am not good enough, I will never succeed	This mistake doesn't determine your life success. Everyone makes mistakes.

Cultivate and Maintain Long-Term Meaningful Relationships

Life without relationships is like playing tug of war but alone! It won't work! Humans are social beings, and relationships are essential to our lives. They provide support, a sense of belonging, security, and safety. Research shows that those with strong relationships are happier, more resilient, live longer, and experience greater life satisfaction.

> Think of relationships like mutual funds. They carry risks but also offer big returns if you invest consistently and wisely. Knowing when to invest more time, effort & resources and when to step back is key to reaping the rewards.

Investing in meaningful relationships:

- Fuels personal growth
- Adds purpose to life
- Boosts happiness and satisfaction
- Enhances overall health and longevity
- Satisfies various psycho-social needs

The 6 important aspects of healthy relationship are:

01 Communication

02 Expression of Love

03 Intimacy (closeness & connection)

04 Conflict resolution

05 Trust & Loyalty

06 Empathy & Understanding

 **To Improve Relationships:**

Improving Communication

01. Practice active listening: Focus fully on the speaker and show that you understand their message.
02. Use "I" statements: Express your feelings and needs without blaming others (e.g., "I feel... when...").
03. Clarify and summarize: Paraphrase what the other person has said to ensure understanding.
04. Provide constructive feedback: Offer feedback that is specific, actionable, and supportive.
05. Avoid interrupting: Let the other person finish speaking before you respond.

Learning to Express Love:

06. Words of Affirmation: Give compliments, express appreciation, and acknowledge others' efforts.
07. Acts of Service: Offer to help with tasks, support others' needs, or do something special for them.
08. Quality Time: Spend uninterrupted, focused time together doing activities you both enjoy.
09. Physical Touch: Use appropriate physical affection such as hugs, kisses, pats on the back, a comforting touch or sexual intimacy.
10. Receiving Gifts: Give thoughtful and meaningful gifts that show you care.

Practicing Empathy and Understanding:

11. Put yourself in others' shoes: Try to understand their perspective and feelings.
12. Show compassion: Respond to others' needs and challenges with kindness.
13. Validate emotions: Acknowledge and accept others' feelings without judgement.
14. Ask questions: Show genuine interest in others' experiences and viewpoints.
15. Be patient: Give others time to express themselves and process their emotions.

Actively Working on Intimacy

16. Share personal stories and experiences to build deeper connections.

17. Express vulnerability: Share your fears, dreams, and insecurities.

18. Create rituals: Establish regular activities or traditions that you do together.

19. Be present: Put away distractions and focus on being in the moment with the other person.

20. Show appreciation: Regularly acknowledge and appreciate the efforts and qualities of others.

Conflict Resolution

21. Address issues promptly: Don't let conflicts fester; address them as they arise.

22. Stay calm and composed: Avoid raising your voice or becoming defensive.

23. Focus on the issue, not the person: Avoid personal attacks and stay on topic.

24. Seek to understand: Try to see the situation from the other person's perspective.

25. Find common ground: Look for solutions that satisfy both parties needs.

Building Trust and Loyalty:

26. Be reliable and consistent: Follow through on promises and commitments.

27. Show integrity: Be honest and ethical in your actions and decisions.

28. Respect confidentiality: Keep private information shared with you confidential.

29. Be supportive: Stand by others in times of need and celebrate their successes.

30. Practice transparency: Be open about your intentions & share relevant information.

Strengthening Relationships

Mark which of the 6 aspects do you need to improve at, with respect to different relationships in your life. Referring to the earlier tips, choose and decide what you would like to implement.

Relationship to Improve	Communication	Love	Understanding	Intimacy	Conflict	Trust	Tips I can Implement
Mom	✓		✓				Ask questions about her day Use "I" statements

 Do Things That Matter to You

Think back to the past week—what kind of activities did you dive into? Were they fun, energizing, inspiring, maybe a little bit relaxing? Or were they more like a never-ending to-do list?

Imagine your daily activities as ingredients in a recipe. For a truly satisfying life, you need to add four key ingredients:

Pleasure	Leisure	Upliftment	Stimulation
Enjoyment, happiness, and satisfaction	Relaxation, rest, and downtime	Energizing and cheering yourself up	Inspiring and intellectually challenging experiences

Skipping any of these ingredients can turn your life's recipe into a bland dish—leaving you with feelings of emptiness, lack of purpose, and higher stress levels. To create a well-balanced life, adjust these ingredients based on what you need each day.

> People who regularly engage in hobbies are 34% more likely to report higher life satisfaction.

> A healthy balance of pleasurable, energizing, inspiring & relaxing activities add a sense of purpose, enhance satisfaction, and improve overall well-being.

> Spending time on activities that matter can reduce the risk of depression by 23%.

 Tip

Make sure that the activities you choose are aligned with your goals and values.

"Doing what you love is the cornerstone of having abundance in your life."

— Wayne Dyer

Healthy Activities Menu Card

Create a flexible menu of activities that you can choose from, depending on your current needs—whether you want to feel energised, relaxed, joyful, or mentally stimulated. List various activities under the appropriate categories. Use symbols/colours/words to represent time, effort, cost needed for the task. Pick activities based on what you need and your available resources. Update your menu as needed.

PLEASURE ₹

Listening to Music (15 mins) — Free

UPLIFTMENT ₹

Morning Jog (30 mins) — Low

STIMULATION ₹

Reading a Book (15 mins) — Low

LEISURE ₹

Cooking a New Recipe (45 mins) — Varies

My Plus Factor

Prioritize pleasure and leisure in your routine by scheduling them according to your needs. Make sure you include them EVERY WEEK.

	PLUS	Activity	Comments
MONDAY			
TUESDAY			
WEDNESDAY			
THURSDAY			
FRIDAY			
SATURDAY			
SUNDAY			

Evaluate Long-Term Costs and Benefits

Do you struggle with "what to order for dinner?"

You're not alone—research shows, we make around 300 decisions just about food, each day! And that's food—imagine the brainpower it takes to make the big life choices!

Decision-making is central to our lives, and while small choices may bring little stress, the big ones often come with confusion, anxiety and sometimes even decision paralysis- an inability to make any decision! We are likely to make regrettable decisions, when under pressure to make positive & right decisions!

"Decisions aren't just about choosing what's better; they're about deciding which struggles you're willing to face for the advantages you want."

Every choice has its own set of struggles. The real question is: Which struggles are worth it E.g. would you endure chemo for a chance at a longer life? Sacrifice family time for career growth? Tolerate smoking to be with your partner?

There are no right or wrong decisions indeed! The choice that seems helpful today might have consequences tomorrow, and vice versa. E.g. Dropping out of college may seem like a "bad idea" but it led Steve Jobs to a career of innovation. Marrying a loving partner still led Angeline Jolie & Brad Pitt into an unhappy marriage

For improved decision making, consider

The Big Picture: How will this decision affect various aspects of your life?
Think about how this decision will impact your overall well-being and future goals.

Time Investment: How much time am I willing to spend on this?
The bigger the decision's impact, the more time it deserves.

Long-Term Focus: Prioritize long-term benefits over short-term ease.
Ask yourself: What long-term advantages or challenges does this decision present compared to immediate gratification?

Balanced View: Evaluate both costs and benefits.
Consider: Am I focusing on the long-term benefits and costs equally, or am I overemphasizing one aspect?

Long-Term vs. Short-Term Analysis

Think of a recent decision you made based on immediate comfort or ease. Now, list the long-term benefits and costs, as well as short-term benefits and costs of that decision. Reflect on how this might influence similar decisions in the future.

Short Term

Benefits   **Costs**

Long Term

Benefits   **Costs**

Focus on the Greys

Ever catch yourself thinking, "If I can't do it perfectly, why bother?" or "If you're not with me, you're against me"? "If she cannot get this done, she's totally incompetent?"

> These types of all-or-nothing thoughts are classic examples of black-and-white thinking—a cognitive distortion that oversimplifies situations & people into extreme, absolute categories. This thinking error makes us judge things as polar opposites —good or bad, always or never, success or failure—ignoring the nuances in between.

Do you think life is really that simplistic and clear cut

Black & white thinking is like watching a movie in just 2 colours- how much detail and depth are you missing out on? In reality, life is more like a full-color spectrum. By embracing the greys, you allow yourself to see things more clearly, which leads to better decisions, improved judgement healthier relationships, and more balanced emotions.

Research shows that black-and-white thinking is linked to procrastination, perfectionism, depression, OCD, and relationship conflicts.

Shifting your focus to the grey areas where most of life actually happens can:

- Reduce procrastination and the pressure of perfectionism.

- Enhance your relationships by fostering better conflict resolution.

- Improve consistency in your actions and decisions.

- Boost your motivation and sense of progress.

- Lead to more balanced and thoughtful decision-making.

All Things Grey

Identify some +ves and -ves for different people and situations in your life.
This will help you recognize that nothing is ever all good or bad.

I received an award

+ves	-ves
Recognition Success Pride, Happiness	Stress Missed social-life Sacrificed Weekends

Break-up

+ves	-ves
Finally over No confusion No fights	Change Sadness, grief Loneliness

+ves	-ves

+ves	-ves

+ves	-ves

+ves	-ves

How Grey Am I?

In the table below write down various aspects of your life E.g relationship with mom, art project, singing skills, weight loss, career performance. Define what "white" and "black" for this category is, and carefully mark your reality accordingly.

Black is for absolute zero and white is perfect
Mark where your reality stands on this scale

Life Events	⚫	⚫	🔘	⚪
MONEY	No earning, Zero Balance	I earned 45k this month		More than 1 Lakh/month
EXAMS	Less than 40%		80%	100%

Get Quality Sleep

Sleep is crucial for your mental and physical well-being. It is a basic biological need such as food, water and oxygen!

Sleep is a basic biological need, as important as food, water and oxygen —and skipping it can kill you faster than going without food. Yet, we're the only mammals who willingly delay it! Sleep isn't just downtime; it's your brain's cleaning crew, body repair squad, and tech support all in one. You burn around 400 calories just by sleeping because your brain is hard at work—utilizing energy for maintenance, upkeep and development of physical and mental functions. It removes toxins, repairs neural pathways, heals your body, builds muscle, regulates glucose, balances hormones, and strengthens your immune system. It's your nightly reset button!

Interesting Sleep facts zzZ

 Women have a lifetime risk of insomnia that is as much as 40% higher than men. Women need more sleep than men yet get less sleep than men!

 Most brain development happens when we sleep. Sleep deprivation during infancy and childhood is linked to mental retardation & developmental delays.

 There are over 80 Recognized Sleep Disorders. Most common ones include: Insomnia, Restless Leg Syndrome, Sleep Apnea, Hypersomnia & Parasomnia.

Given below are the characteristics of healthy sleep. Do a quick sleep check up for yourself by marking the criteria you met last night.

- [ ] **Got 7-8 hours of sleep**
- [ ] **Got 5 hours of sun-down sleep (Slept no later than 1:00 AM)**
- [ ] **Fell asleep within 30 minutes of going to bed**
- [ ] **Fell asleep without any substance or stimulus (alcohol, meds or other drugs)**
- [ ] **Got uninterrupted sleep (woke up no more than once at night)**
- [ ] **Fell back asleep within 20 minutes if you did wake up**
- [ ] **Felt rested upon waking up**
- [ ] **Maintained consistent sleep schedule (same bed-time & wake-up time)**
- [ ] **Slept & woke up naturally & not forcefully**

Sleeping extra to compensate for sleep doesn't help. Damage from lack of sleep is permanent

Body does not get used to a lack of sleep. You cannot train your body to need less sleep.

Impacts of Poor Sleep

Productivity

- Leads to low energy, lethargy
- low motivation & increased procrastination
- Reduced attention, alertness & focus
- Worsens response time, speed & accuracy
- Affects Information processing & Learning
- Causes memory lapses & issues with retrieval & recall
- Leads to confusion, brain fog & lack of Clarity
- Issues with reasoning, decision making, judgement
- Affects problem solving

Mental health

- Lead to onset & worsening of mental health issues
- Linked to depression, anxiety, risk taking behaviour and suicidal ideation
- Reduces frustration tolerance & adjustment
- Impacts mood & emotional regulation
- Affects being in the present
- Causes issues with self regulation, impulsivity & self control
- Increased stress
- Increased irritability

Physical Health

- Disrupts the body's hunger hormone (leptin), leading weight gain
- Increases cravings for high-calorie foods
- Reduces Pain tolerance
- Linked to heart disease and stroke
- Increased risk of diabetes
- Chronic fatigue
- Tiredness
- Drowsiness
- Reduced energy levels
- Day-time sleepiness

PRIORITISE SLEEP

- Learn about sleep
- Recognize your sleep patterns & problems (Identify areas of improvement)
- Consciously and intentionally commit to improving your sleep
- Schedule and plan sleep (Know what to do and when)
- Implement one thing at a time and make gradual changes
- Give yourself permission to fail and try again
- Seek Help if you need to!

GENERAL DAILY HABITS

- Fix your bed-time (Use alarms & reminders to prepare yourself for sleep)
- Wake up at the same time everyday (even on weekends)
- Start a sleep diary to track what affects your rest
- Exercise at least 20 minutes each day, but try to do it at least 4 hours before bedtime
- Make sure you are fulfilled in the day (Meet your social, intellectual, physical & personal needs)
- Learn ways to manage your emotions, stress (Overthinking is the greatest cause of sleep disturbances)
- Use bed only for S: Sleep, Sex, Sickness (no eating, working or studying on the bed)
- Keep yourself healthy and fit (Physical pains & discomfort are linked to poor sleep)

THINGS TO AVOID

- At bedtime: Mental activities that are engaging & stimulating (Talking about stressful or emotional issues, planning, Social Media, Working etc can interfere with winding down)
- 1 hour before bedtime: Screens (Light affects melatonin levels)
- 2 hours before bedtime : Meals (Spicy foods & big meals cause acidity & distress)
- 3 hrs before bedtime: Alcohol & Nicotine (Stimulants cause sleep disturbances)
- 4 hrs before bedtime: Rigorous exercise (Endorphins from working lead to arousal)
- 7 hours before bed-time: Caffeine (stimulant cause sleep disturbances)
- Day time napping (If you nap, keep it short- 20-30 minutes, and not close to bedtime.)

BED-TIME ROUTINE

- Prepare to wind down (Use an alarm or reminder 1 or 2 hours before bed-time)
- Nothing exciting after this (No screen, food, work, substances or activating tasks after this)
- Get ready for bed (Personal night tasks & rituals: washup, change, use the washroom etc)
- Prepare the room (Clutter free bed, cool temperature, dim lights, no noise)
- Engage in relaxing activities: Light music, stretching, relaxation & breathing exercises, meditation, reading, colouring, journaling etc

The Goodnight Ritual

Establish a calming pre sleep routine incorporating activities like: reading or gentle stretching to signal your body that it's time to wind down.

Sample Sleep Routine

ACTIVITY	TIME	DETAILS
Nothing new (Reminder)	9:45 PM	Can't start a new episode post this, Dim the lights
Wind down (Alarm	10:15 PM	Screens away, Start routine
Clean up		Wind up kitchen, put dishes away
Prep for next day	10:30 PM	Soak almonds, decide breakfast
Ready for bed		Get water, use washroom, freshen up, change, skin care
Bedtime activty	11:00 pm	30 mins: Journaling or colouring or reading (mood based)
If cant sleep		Read Practitioners guide, Progressive muscle relaxation

Your Sleep Routine

ACTIVITY	TIME	DETAILS

Sleep Tracker

Use the tracker below to keep a check if you have been sleeping well by tracking items on the sleep checklist. Alternatively, you can use it, to track the sleep hygiene habits you wish to try!

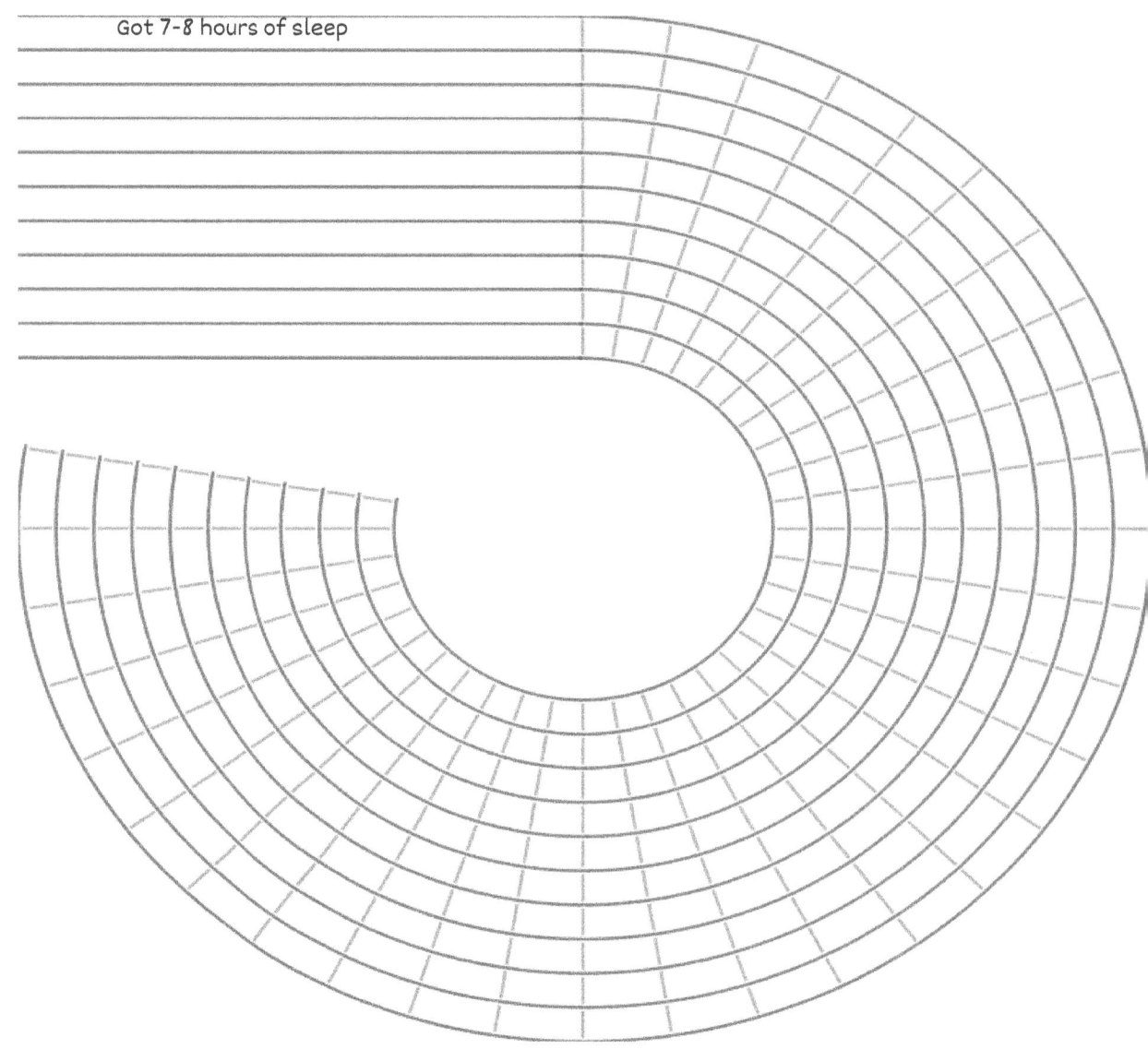

Got 7-8 hours of sleep

Have Realistic Expectation

Do you want to be rich or hope for the world to be better or wish that your parents truly understood you?

We all have expectations— desires from ourselves, others, and life. Expectations serve as baselines. We are pleased when they are met and disappointed when they aren't fulfilled.

Expectations are ideas that are responsible for our emotions. While expectations drive us, problems arise when they turn into rigid demands, identified by words like "should" or "must"

Such demands lead to:

- Believe that your wish must be fulfilled at any cost.
- Be blinded towards the realistic chance of disappointment.
- Not consider a margin of error in outcomes & possibilities.

There are 3 musts that hold us back
1. I must do well. 2. You must treat me well 3. World must be easy

-Albert Ellis

Demands from self	Demands from others	Demands from life/world
I should do my best	He should care for me	This should not be so hard
I should perform well	My wife should understand me	Life should not be so unfair
I should not hurt others	They should not lie to me	My life should be comfortable
I must not fail	My brother must not ignore me	Things should go well

Flexible realistic expectations encourages acceptance, improves preparedness and makes it easier to adapt to change, whereas rigid demands are

1. Unhelpful, harmful & illogical

2. Create stress & lead to emotional distress

3. Increases pressure, leads to frustration, and contributes to negative thoughts

4. Impacts relationship and communication

Expectations v/s Outcome

Write down various expectations that you have from yourself, others and life. Use different colours to denote whether they were met or not. Mark the outcome in the boxes corresponding to these expectations. Do this as often as you can!

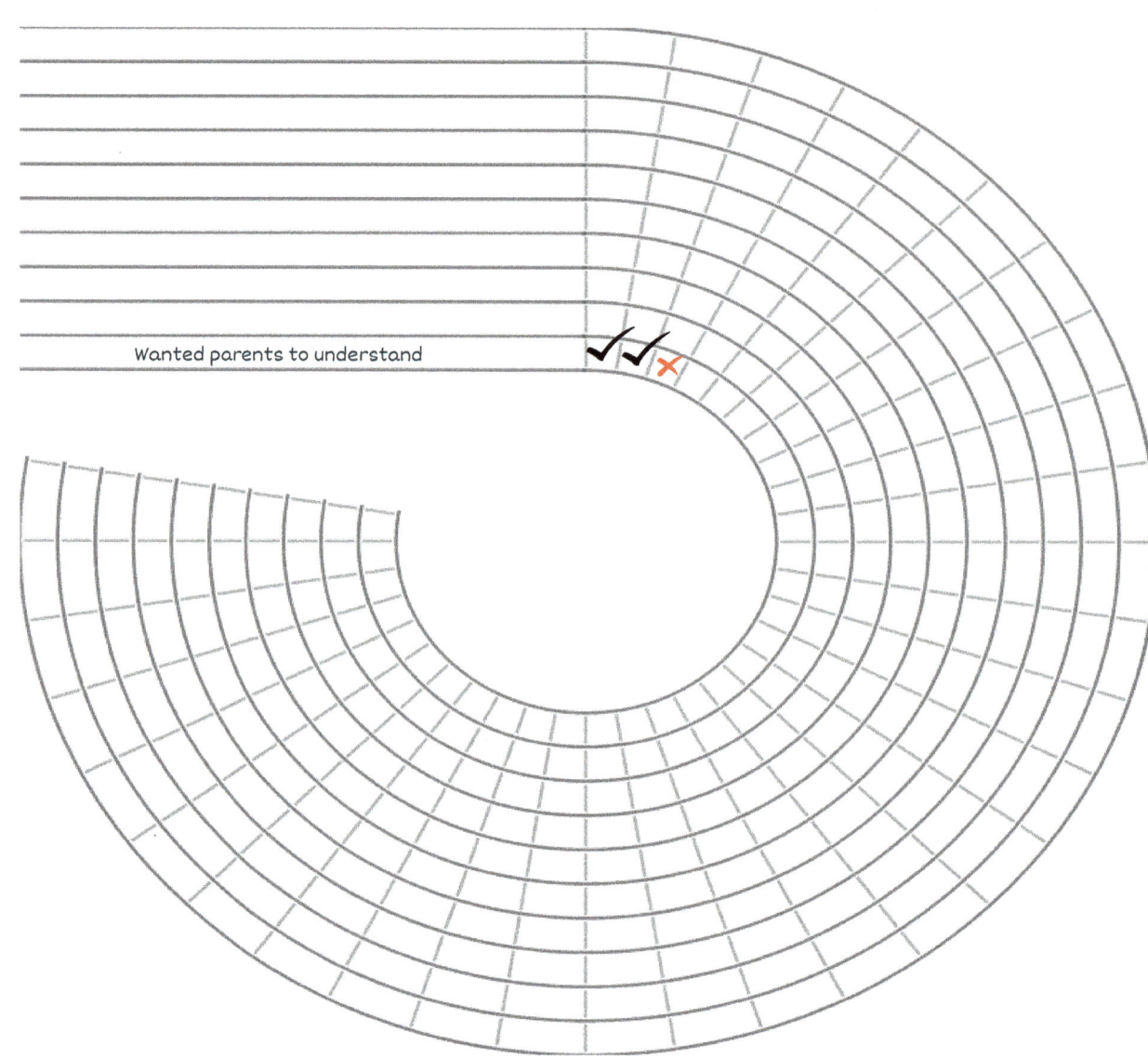

Challenging "Shoulds"

Answer the following questions for your demands- "should" & "must" thoughts

My demand: _____

- **What is the evidence that my expectation will definitely come true?**
  ....
  ....
  ....

- **What is the evidence that my expectation may not come true?**
  ....
  ....
  ....

- **What are the other possible outcomes that are possible?**
  ....
  ....
  ....

- **What steps can I take to increase the chances of my preferred outcome?**
  ....
  ....
  ....

- **What can I do if my expectation is not met?**
  ....
  ....
  ....

Improve Your Tolerance

Sounds familiar? You may have gone through breakups, boring lectures, or even grief with a similar experience! We often overestimate discomfort and underestimate our ability to handle it. This error not only makes us avoid discomfort and sabotage growth but it also makes the process and experience more difficult than it may be!

Constantly focusing on how uncomfortable something is makes it harder to get through making it difficult for us to achieve our goals. Although it is natural to resist and difficult to deal with discomfort, pushing through is often the only way to reach our goals.

All growth happens upon stepping outside your comfort zone!

– Wayne Dyer

Whether it's pushing through emotional pain after a fight, enduring the physical strain of exercise, or dealing with frustrating paperwork, discomfort is inevitable and tolerating it, necessary for growth.

> I wonder if there is a single human alive who has never experienced discomfort at all? That's impossible! After all, staying alive starts with crying at birth!

Discomfort is, quite literally, the foundation of survival.
And survival is naturally uncomfortable.

When life is bound to throw discomfort your way, the real question is: How much can you truly handle? What's your limit?

How many people need to judge you for you to get a heart attack?

How many uncomfortable conversations before you disintegrate?

How many boring tasks before you crumble?

> You'd be surprised at the immense capacity humans have to bear discomfort. The reality is, **discomfort can't kill us**—but telling yourself "I can't handle this" not only makes life harder, it's simply not true.
>
> It's a lie that magnifies your discomfort. If things are going to be tough anyway, the solution may be building resilience & powering through.

Think of it like upgrading the fuse for a new appliance. The old one blows with high load, but the upgraded one can take greater pressure.

Similarly, Upgrading your tolerance lets you handle life's challenges with less energy wasted on discomfort. It leads you to -

- Stay focused and resilient
- Take effective action
- Maintain motivation
- Work steadily toward your goals
- Accept & overcome challenges

Affirmations to Improve Toleranc

> *"This may be very difficult, even painful, but I can tolerate it! I have the capacity to endure this!"*

> *"I have lived through many discomforts. Powering through this is worth it for my goal"*

Pain is Gain

Reflect & write down answers to the following questions about a frustrating situation you are finding difficult to tolerate.

The Frustrating situation:

Reasons why pushing through & persisting this is worth it?

Past situations when I managed to do bare discomfort?

How has pushing my comfort zone & enduring this helped in the past?

How will upgrading my tolerance fuse help me?

Endure & Conquer

For an upcoming task you're dreading, write down your expected discomfort. Then, reflect on times when you successfully endured similar challenges. These are those majestic moments that led you to succeed!

TASK: *Studying for a professional certification*

What discomforts am I expecting?

Giving up morning time, Less time to myself Disturbance in routine, Work-life balance going off, Not being able to chill

When & how have I endured similar challenges?

During the initial years of my business & my student years. I knew I had to do it. There was no other way to grow and get what I wanted

TASK:

What discomforts am I expecting?

When & how have I endured similar challenges?

#PracticalExperiment

Identify one thing every week to push yourself outside your comfort zone. Apply this in various areas of your life!

Jot Down Your Strengths

We've all been there, whether in therapy or not. Somehow, it's always easier to spot our weaknesses while our strengths seem to stay hidden in plain sight. It's like we're hardwired to focus on what's wrong rather than what's right. But mental health work isn't just about patching potholes & avoiding crashes, it's also about developing faster and smoother highways! And your strengths are the bricks to personal development.

Character Strengths: Traits that are core to you like kindness, perseverance & curiosity.

Performance Strengths: Your ability to tackle & excel at tasks in various areas of life!

Why focus on strengths ?

✓ When you recognize your strengths, you can channel them to create ease and success into every aspect of life—relationships, career, personal challenges.

✓ Strengths improve resilience, boost confidence & enhance performance.

How to Identify Your Strengths:

01 Reflection
Recall past successes and what you're proud of.

02 Scientific Tests
Tools like the VIA Character Strengths Survey

03 Feedback
Ask friends or colleagues—they often see strengths you might overlook.

04 Evidence
Look at patterns in your achievements and positive feedback.

My Superpowers

Use reflection, feedback & evidence to enlist your strengths using the prompts

Skills

Good Performance, Success, Achievements

Personal Characteristics & Qualities

People around whom I am my best (add value)

My Resources

My Superpowers

Use reflection, feedback & evidence to enlist your strengths using the prompts

Talents
+VE Feedback, appreciation received
Interests & Passions
My conducive Environments
My Past learnings

Know and Tame Your Stress

Stress is like that annoying alarm that won't stop ringing until you hit "snooze." It's is our (mental & physical) response to challenges and demands. It is natural and common but can become unhealthy when it upsets your day-to-day functioning.

- **About 50% of all doctors visits are stress related**
- **Women experience greater stress than men**
- **Stress is linked to autoimmune disorders, hormonal imbalances, coronary heart disease, weakened immune system, and overall mental health.**
- **Stress management improves physical and mental health.**

Signs of Stress:

- **Physical Symptoms:** Headaches, muscle tension, fatigue, gut issues (acidity, constipation), frequent infections & allergies, changes in appetite, lowered sex drive
- **Emotional Symptoms:** Anxiety, mood swings, irritability, outbursts, flash anger, hopelessness, numbness & indifference
- **Behavioral Symptoms:** Changes in sleep, social withdrawal, over or under eating, substance use, avoidance & procrastination
- **Cognitive Symptoms:** Difficulty concentrating, racing thoughts, forgetfulness, brain fog & confusion, problems with decision making & judgement

Source of Stress:

Environmental	Noise, weather, temperature, pollution, traffic; social, cultural & political environment; pandemic, terrorist attacks, natural disasters etc
Physiological	Health & fitness related issues like disabilities, disease/illness, infection/allergy, disorders, pains, injuries, reproductive health etc.
Social	Social & Interpersonal issues like rejection, conflicts, disagreements, breakups, societal pressures, judgments, communication problems, relationship issues etc
Psychological	Irrational thoughts, attitudes, beliefs; emotional distress, unhealthy habits & behaviours, decisions, confusion, personal pressures & conflicts etc

> Stress management like is hitting that snooze button before the alarm blares on full blast!

Here are some techniques to try for stress management.

Skills To Improve

- Rational Thinking
- Emotional Regulation
- Self Awareness
- Effective Communication
- Relationship management
- Time Management
- Overcoming Procrastination
- Goal Setting & Planning
- Progressive Muscle Relaxation
- Deep Breathing

Things to Try

- Journaling
- Yoga & Meditation
- Gratitude
- Mindfulness
- Therapy

Everyday Basics

- Creative Visualization
- Healthy diet
- Exercise
- Balanced Lifestyle
- Sleep Hygiene
- Self Care
- Social Engagement
- Limiting Screen time
- Avoiding Substances

Goodbye Stress

Refer to the above information & help yourself identify your stress pattern and strategies! In the table, write down your personal stressors, the signs of stress you experience, identify the type of stressor for each situation and note the strategy that can help you.

Stressor	Signs & Symptoms	Source of stress	Solution I can try
Family doesn't give me space	Headache, irritability, too much instagram	Social	Assertiveness & boundaries balanced lifestyle emotional regulation

Tip — Avoid situations that trigger stress (consider long term impact) E.g. Avoiding Social media & news if that triggers you, breaking up or drawing boundaries with difficult people, give up chasing goals that are not worth it.

Look at Life as a Whole

What makes up your life? Is it your work, relationships, hobbies—or is it all of these things together?

Life isn't just one piece; it's a mosaic, with each part contributing to the whole.

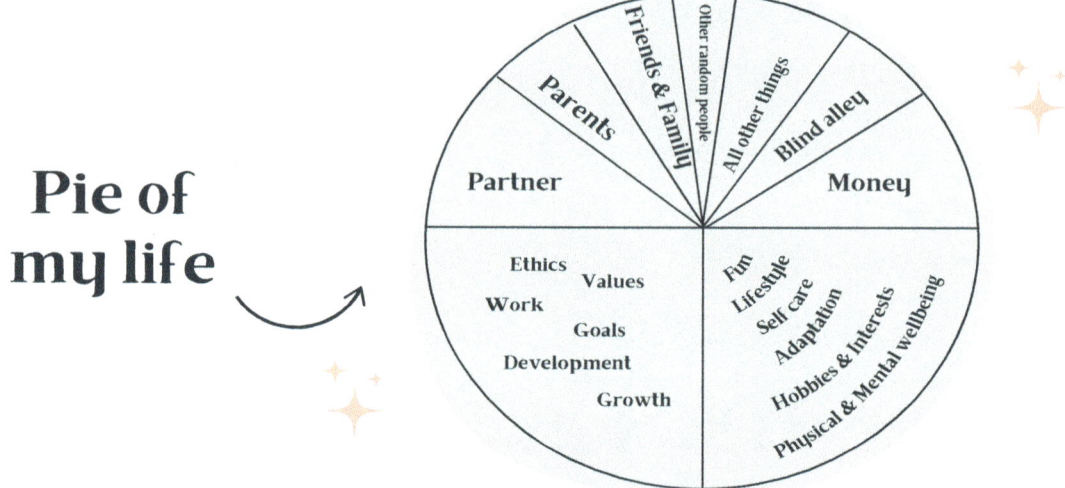

Yet, how often have you zoomed in on just one piece—like your relationship or career—and made sweeping judgments: "Without love, my life is meaningless!" "If I can't find my passion, what's the point?" "If I can't walk, my life is over."

We all fall into this trap—focusing on one negative aspect and losing sight of the bigger picture. This narrow perspective makes us forget the bigger picture, leading to stress, dissatisfaction, and hopelessness. It overshadows the good in our lives, making us devalue things that truly matter.

Here's the truth: no single part of your life, no matter how important, can define or destroy the rest. A broken pipe doesn't make your house unlivable, just like a breakup can't erase your friendships, health, or achievements. The key is to zoom out and view life as a whole. This shift in perspective helps you navigate life's ups and downs with greater resilience.

Affirmations

"My life is made up of many valuable aspects; it can never be defined by one alone."

"One aspect, even significant, cannot define my entire life."

"My life is like a sitcom or a book - It can't be judged to a single chapter or episode; it's the entire story that matters."

Life's a Pie

Create a pie chart representing different aspects of your life. The area they take up will depend on the importance they carry in your life. Make sure to represent aspects like relationships, health, career, hobbies, etc.

- How much of my time, energy, mental space, effort am I giving to various aspects of my life and how much attention should I really be giving?

....
....

- Which areas of my life do I tend to overlook? How can I nurture those areas more?

....
....

 Maintain a Balanced Life

Ever feel like you're juggling 100 things and dropping them all? Or like a phone running 20 apps at once, slowly crashing? That's what life looks like without balance!

Ask yourself:

Do you actually make time for self-care and hobbies?	YES / NO
Can you balance work and personal goals without losing your mind?	YES / NO
Are you able to prioritize exercise, sleep, and nutrition consistently?	YES / NO

If you answered NO to any of these, you're probably struggling to keep balance —and it's okay, many of us are!

A balanced life is about making choices that support your overall well-being. It means finding the sweet spot between different areas of life:

- **Physical Health:** Proper sleep, diet, exercise, hygiene (yes, showering counts!).
- **Social Life:** Maintaining relationships with family, friends, colleagues—no, texting memes doesn't count as "catching up."
- **Productivity:** Work, studies, chores, and personal growth.
- **Pleasure:** Hobbies and activities that light you up!
- **Leisure:** Downtime, Netflix binges, or a good old nap.
- **Mental Health:** Managing stress, practicing self-awareness, and ensuring psychological well-being.

An Imbalanced life can lead to:

Stress, frustration, conflict due to unmet needs
Loneliness and isolation
Poor health and a shorter lifespan
FOMO and existential dread (like the whole "What am I doing with my life?" spiral)
Loss of joy and life satisfaction

Time Detective

Use the below 24 hour clock and fill in with details of how you spend your time. You can alternatively keep a note of your 24 hours in an excel sheet, a diary, your phone or a tracking app on your device. Track this for 7 typical days of your life to recognise your patterns. Alternatively you can also make and use your own key to track the following necessary lifestyle.

- Physical health & fitness
- Social Life
- Engagement
- Pleasure
- Leisure
- Mental Health

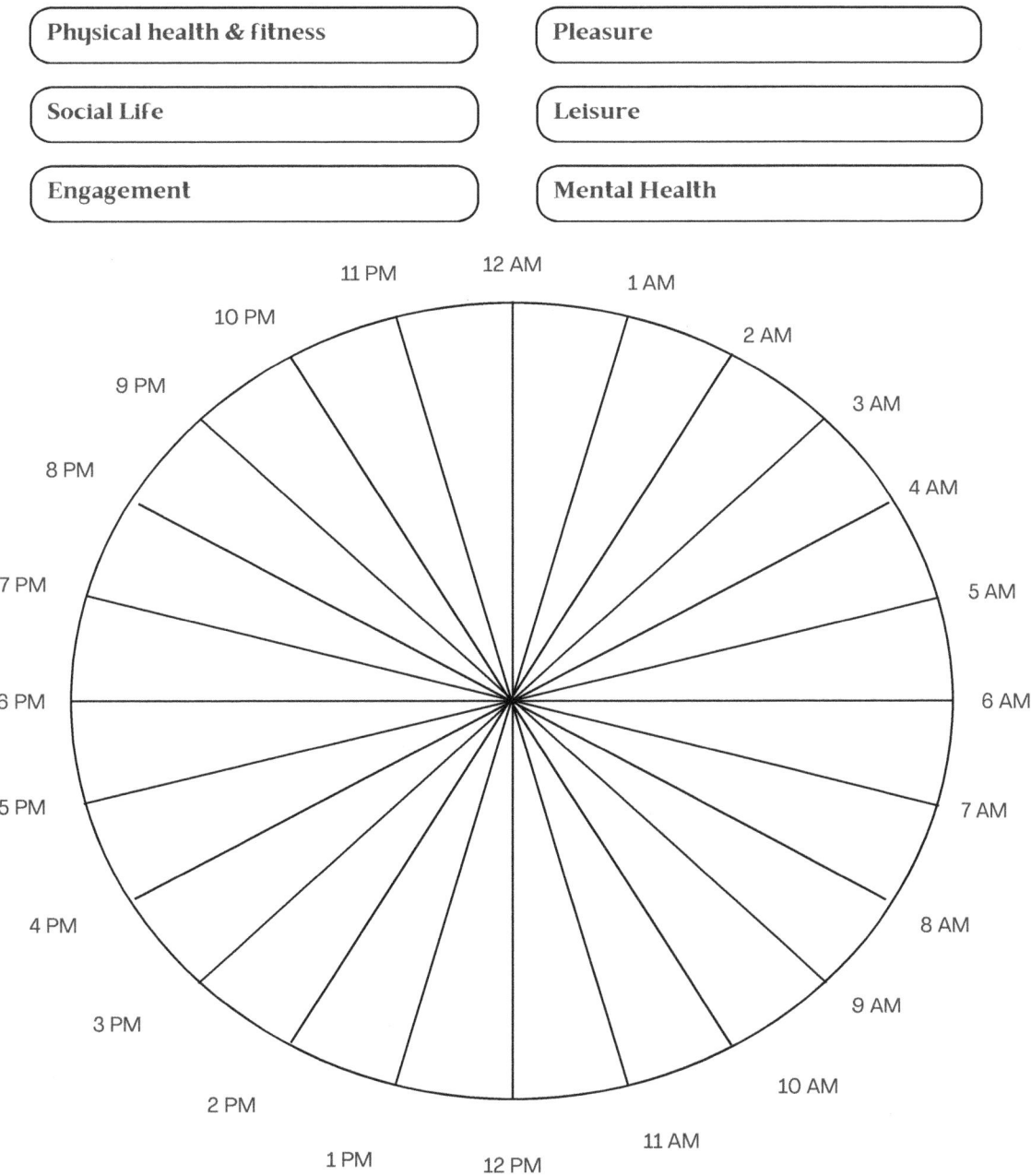

Audit Your lifestyle

Here is a list of the aspects that need to be a part of your lifestyle. Fill in your reality from 1st exercise and identify where you are with regard to each of these aspects. Find out the problems & determine the action you need to take. Adjust this according to to your unique life demands, challenges while referring to the ideal lifestyle guide.

Important aspects of a healthy lifestyle	Healthy/ balanced time	How much time do I spend	What action Do I need to take?
Sleep	8 hours		
3 Meals	1.5 hours		
Hygiene	1 hour		
Productivity (school/work)	7.5 hour		
Digital/ Technology (Netflix, social media)	1 hour		
Chores and responsibilities	1 hour		
Exercise	1 hour		
Social relationships (birthdays, outings, parties)	1 hour		
Self-care (therapy, relaxation, hobbies, skill building, etc)	1 hour		
Buffer time	1 hour		

Navigate through Your Emotions

Emotions—those powerful waves of feelings that hit us when life happens! They show up in all shapes and sizes, and understanding them helps you navigate life's highs and lows. Emotions are reactions to events or situations. They involve three key components:

Physiological Changes:
Your body's response (e.g., racing heart, sweaty palms).

Subjective Experience:
How you personally interpret the emotion (e.g., "I'm nervous,"

Behavioral Response:
The actions or expressions that follow (e.g., crying, laughing).

Every time you feel an emotion, it's a unique combination of these components. This creates two key complexities:

1. Individual Differences: People may experience the same emotion differently. For example, two people feeling guilty about forgetting their mom's birthday might react in opposite ways—one might over-apologize, while the other avoids the issue completely.

2. Situational Variability: Even within the same person, emotions can change based on context. You might feel anxiety as fidgeting and sweating before a presentation, but as agitation and micromanagement during a work project.

With so many emotions and such complexities, it's natural to struggle with navigating them. In a world where most can't even name emotions, let's help you decode through them!

Think of emotions as a traffic signal—each has a purpose in guiding you.

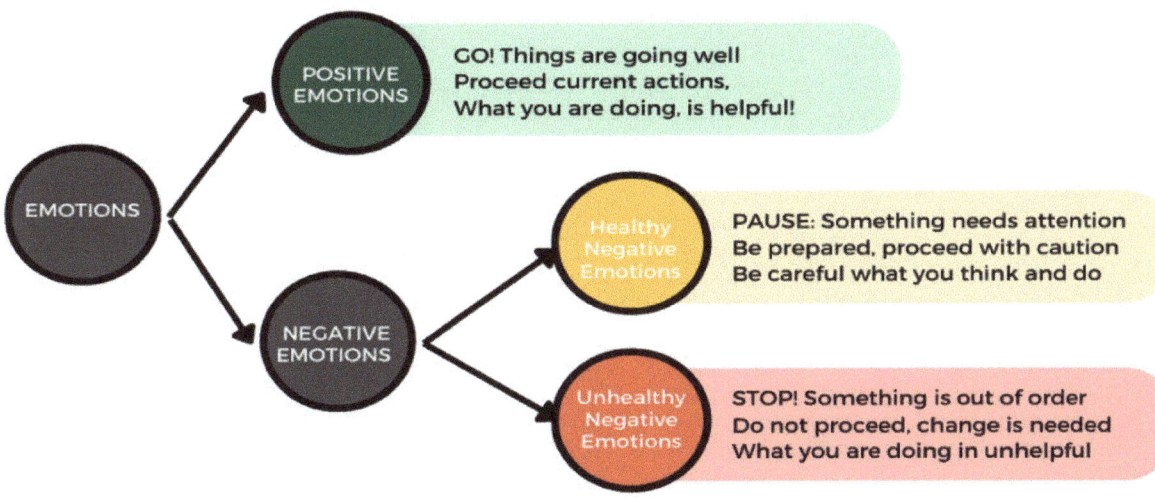

43

Signal: something is out of order
- Unhelpful, dysfunctional, disturbing
- Unnecessary, Counterproductive
- Hijacks thought, sabotaging action
- Inappropriate, exaggerated

Signal: Something needs attention
- Helpful, Functional,
- Necessary
- Motivate to adapt & solve problem
- Relevant, appropriate, proportional

UNHEALTHY

Hurt, Guilt, Shame, Anxiety, Depression, Envy, Anger, Jealousy

HEALTHY

Disappointment, Scared, Nervous, Regret, Remorse, Sadness, Upset, Annoyance

NEGATIVE EMOTIONS
Show up in Adversities
Undesirable, Uncomfortable
Want to avoid & get rid of them

POSITIVE EMOTIONS
Show up in "good" situations
We Crave & chase them
Desirable, comfortable
Reinforce & Motivate us

POSITIVE EMOTIONS

Love, Pride, Satisfaction, Happiness, Excitement, Gratitude

UNE Checklist

- ☐ Clouded my judgment
- ☐ Led to overthinking
- ☐ Lasted & troubled for a long time
- ☐ Caused physical distress
- ☐ Led to ineffective, unproductive or unhealthy actions/behaviors
- ☐ Affected my ability & capacity to function
- ☐ Disturbed, troubled or hijacked me

All emotions, irrespective of their nature, are valid and justified. However, not all are healthy & relevant! Use your emotions as signals to decide when to slow down, keep going, or stop and reassess!

What Am I feeling?

Write down incidents that you feel strongly about. Identify if these are Positive Emotions, Healthy Negative Emotions (HNE) or Unhealthy Negative Emotions (UNE). Use the Emotions Guide to help you differentiate among them. Decide your own color to represent the below mentioned emotions

○ **Unhealthy Negative Emotion**   ○ **Healthy Negative Emotion**   ○ **Positive Emotion**

When?	Incident?	Emo key
Friday	BIG Promotion	○
Saturday	Dad and I had an argument	○
		○
		○
		○
		○
		○
		○
		○
		○
		○
		○
		○

Unpacking Emotions

Fill this page only for your unhealthy negative emotions so you can identify your patterns and the links between your emotions, reactions & outcomes.

Situation (What happened? when?)	Feeling (One word, name or intensity)	Physical sensations (What/how I felt in the body)	Reaction/ Action (What I did or didn't do)	Outcomes (How does this impact others, you & the situation in long term?)
Didn't know answer to boss's question	Anxiety (7)	Heart rate up short breath nervous	Said irrelevant things became defensive	Affect performance

Overcome Fear of Judgement

Do you ever feel like you're constantly under the microscope? Like people are judging how you look, talk, or act? Well, you're definitely not alone!

Anxiety about judgment affects everyone. While it's normal to care about others' opinions (we do have to coexist, after all), overthinking it can hijack your freedom. Thoughts like "What are people going to think of me?" "What if they don't like me?" "He will think I am a loser!" "I will look stupid" are like parasites —they latch onto your mind and stop you from living fully!

Caring too much about what others think can lead to-

- Decisions that don't align with your values or goals
- Limited self expression, missed opportunities
- Feeling out of touch with yourself
- Frustration, dissatisfaction & distress
- Internal conflict, confusion, and self-doubt

It's like letting someone else hold the remote to your life—you're watching their show instead of starring in your own!

But here's the truth: Are you really the star of their life? Most people are too busy starring in their own shows to focus on you!

When was the last time you obsessed over what someone wore two days ago?

Overcoming the fear of judgement isn't about ignoring others; it's about choosing your own values over someone else's opinion.

Based on the assumptions that:

- People thinking about me
- They mean something about me
- They are definitely judging me negatively
- They will impact me negatively
- Their negative judgments are true
- I can avoid being judged

Me vs What People Think

Assumption: People are thinking about me

How do I know that they are definitely thinking about me? Is there a possibility that they aren't really thinking about me? Do others really have the time & energy to think about me so much?

_____
_____
_____
_____

Assumption: They are definitely judging me negatively

How do I know that they are definitely judging me negatively? Are there other outcomes apart from -ve judgement? What' the point of assuming that they are thinking badly about me?

_____
_____
_____
_____

Assumption: Their negative judgments are true

Are their judgments facts or opinions? Are opinions personal & subjective or are they absolutely true? Can opinions change?

_____
_____
_____
_____

Me vs What People Think

Assumption: Their opinions mean something about me

When someone has an opinion that chocolate is bad, what does that mean about chocolate? Do other people's opinions really reflect reality? Should they be trusted blindly?

_____
_____
_____
_____
_____

Assumption: Their judgments will lead to horrible consequences

What is the worst thing that can happen if they judge me negatively? How realistic it is for the worst thing to actually happen? What are the chances? Is it humanly possible to tolerate and overcome this outcome?

_____
_____
_____
_____
_____

Assumption: I can avoid being judged

Do you have an immunity against judgement? Is there any human on the planet who is not judged? How can you avoid judgment?

_____
_____
_____
_____
_____

Practice Self Regulation

Relatable?

We've all had our own share of failures when it comes to self-control. Whether it's binge-watching, midnight snacking, or "I'll quit tomorrow" promises, self-regulation is the key to breaking this cycle. t's like having the pause button on a remote during life's intense moments. Hit the pause, the moment things are about to go badly, choose what the character (you) should do next, and play!

It is your superpower to...

- Manage emotions, thoughts, & actions to meet goals
- Stay healthy and aligned with your values
- Make better decisions, even in tough moments

Common things that hard regulate/control

- Controlling temptations: Saying no to something risky e.g. sex without a condom
- Pausing during urges: Stopping yourself from impulsive reaction e.g. lashing out in anger
- Deferring gratification: Delaying fulfilling desires e.g. Waiting for sale instead of splurging now

Lack of self control can have serious repercussions on health, productivity, work, relationships, and finances. It leads to counterproductive actions & causes feelings of guilt, shame & self dislike

Impulse Tracker

Track instances where you resisted or gave in to instant gratification. Reflect on what helped you control your impulses or what led you to give in

Give yourself a star if you resisted instant gratification, a sad face if you gave in, or any mark that feels right to you.

Incident		What helped to control/What led to giving in
Did not text after 11pm	☆	Reminded myself that tomorrow will be fucked, put my phone on auto-sleep mode at 11
Binge watched netflix	☹	Told myself "one episode won't be so bad"
	☐	
	☐	
	☐	
	☐	
	☐	
	☐	
	☐	
	☐	
	☐	
	☐	
	☐	
	☐	

Roadmap to Self Monitoring

Regularly check & record your self regulation pattern by answering the following questions.

What urges do you find difficult to resist?	**Under what circumstances are you more likely to give in?** Mental, physical, emotional states, specific time, alone or with others etc	Solutions to try
Ordering food or eating out	Always dinner time (Post 7:00PM) Dissatisfying day; PMS; No pre-planned dinner idea, Can't think of menu, ingredients not available	"Eat responsibly" alarm at 7:15pm, fix dinner menu & order ingredients in the morning

Conscious Action: After consciously Identifying your pattern you will be able to recognize the moment when you need to intervene. In this moment

Pause → Remind yourself of your long term goal

Track this success ← Reward yourself ← Take desired action

Question Your Thoughts

Every day, our minds produce millions of thoughts in the form of ideas, images, memories, or statements. They're the building blocks of everything we do—thinking, learning, decision-making, problem-solving, and more. Without them, we wouldn't be able to make sense of or interact with the world.

Some thoughts are deliberate and conscious—like remembering what you had for dinner last night—while others are automatic and unconscious, like "This smells great!" or "It's too hard." Irrespective of their nature, thoughts can be either logical or illogical.

Here is a checklist to identify your logical & illogical thought:

Logical (Neither +ve nor -ve)
- ✓ Realistic, factual and true
- ✓ Helpful, functional, healthy
- ✓ Lead to appropriate, relevant & balanced emotions
- ✓ Drive healthy, goal oriented actions
- ✓ Rational: Neither positive nor negative

Illogical (can be either +ve or -ve)
- ✓ Unrealistic, assumptions/opinions
- ✓ Unhelpful, dysfunctional, unhealthy
- ✓ Lead to inappropriate & exaggerated emotions
- ✓ Cause unhealthy, counter productive actions
- ✓ Can be positive or negative

Types of Thoughts

Negative
- False sense of doom
- Lack of hoping
- Underestimating coping abilities
- Inaction or excessive action

Rational
- Accurately estimating threats while being hopeful
- Embracing negative emotion while taking appropriate action

Positive
- Unrealistic and false hope
- Underestimating threats
- Suppressing negative emotions

Research shows...

That challenging negative or distorted thoughts can reduce emotional distress. In fact, this is a core element of Cognitive Behavioral Therapy (CBT), where therapists help you recognize, challenge, and replace illogical thoughts.

Sort my Thoughts

Mentioned below are some thoughts. Identify whether they are positive, negative or rational by marking your response in the +, - & = columns respectively.

#	Thoughts	+	-	=
1	I will never be successful	☐	☐	☐
2	I don't know if I will be successful, but I could be	☐	☐	☐
3	Everything will turn out fine	☐	☐	☐
4	This is too hard, I can't do it	☐	☐	☐
5	Nothing bad will happen	☐	☐	☐
6	This is surely hard, but I have done difficult things before	☐	☐	☐
7	I have failed but I have also succeeded.	☐	☐	☐
8	I am a failure	☐	☐	☐
9	I am the best, I can't fail	☐	☐	☐

Statements 9, 3, 5 are + Positive
Statements 1, 4, 8 are - Negative
Statements 2, 6, 7 are = Rational

Identify Your Thoughts

#	Thoughts	+	-	=
1		☐	☐	☐
2		☐	☐	☐
3		☐	☐	☐
4		☐	☐	☐
5		☐	☐	☐
6		☐	☐	☐
7		☐	☐	☐
8		☐	☐	☐
9		☐	☐	☐

Challenge Your Thought

| Increases Happiness? | Takes me to goal? | Increases Frustration? | Fact or Assumption? |

Is this thinking really useful? **YES   NO**   Should I really keep this thought? **YES   NO**

Will 100 people agree to what I'm thinking? Why?

What are the disadvantages of thinking this way?

| What/ would you say to your loved one if he/she is in the same situation? | What are other possible conclusions apart from my own thought? |

| What evidence do I have for my thought? | Evidence do I have against my thought? |

| Do I have resources that will help me deal with this situation? | Is there absolutely no way in this universe that I could change my thought? |

| Is my thought really logical? Why? | Will this still matter 5 years from now? |

What could you think instead?

How true does this make my original thought? _____%

Studies show that people who regularly engage in thought questioning exercises experience reduced anxiety and better emotional control.

Recognise Your Role in Your Distress

Have you ever been upset? YES / NO

Have you ever over-thought about this upset for hours and made it worse? YES / NO

People don't just get upset, they contribute to their upsetness. - Albert Ellis

How we think, feel, and act plays a significant role in causing, maintaining, and increasing our distress. E.g We upset ourselves by thinking "nothing will ever work out", we make things worse by shouting when angry, we perform badly when we procrastinate.

Sure, people & situations can be challenging, but here's a game-changer: Identifying what YOU are doing to add or maintain your distress is the only thing you can control!

> It's like spilling coffee on your shirt—you can't undo the spill, but you can identify if you did something to cause it & you can choose how you react: wipe it off and move on, or spiral into frustration. Taking responsibility for your role in distress is the first step to regaining control.

> This won't magically fix tough situations, but it will help you navigate them with a lot less stress. It may also help you influence & avoid problematic situations. Taking responsibility for your role in your distress is crucial for creating change.

Take Responsibility

Identify a recent situation where you felt distressed. Think and document your thoughts, emotions and actions that contributed to your distress. Reflect about the role you played in your distress.

Distressing situation	My role in my distress
I have too many things to do and no one helps me. I am always tired.	I don't say no to requests & take on too much. I don't communicate about my difficulties and keep expecting that others should help me. I don't ask for help.
My partner blamed me. We fought and haven't been talking for 2 days.	I yelled, became defensive & pointed out her mistakes instead of listening and taking feedback. I haven't initiated conversation and am letting my ego come in the way.
I am not sleeping well and am very tired all the time.	I keep using my phone at night and don't really follow healthy sleep habits.

> *The best years of your life are the ones in which you decide your problems are your own. You do not blame them on your mother, the ecology, or the president. You realise that you control your own destiny!*
>
> – Albert Ellis

Identify the Better

Choose one unhealthy thought, emotion or habit you've identified. Write down an ideal response you would like. Mention what kind of thoughts, emotions and actions would be helpful. Track your progress over a month to see how your distress levels change.

An unhealthy thought/ emotion or habit:

....
....
....

Your Ideal response: What thoughts, emotions, actions would help instead?

....
....
....
....

Track your progress over a month in the graph given below to see whether your distress levels changes.

Y-axis: INTENSITY (1–10)
X-axis: DAYS (1–31)

Seek Help When Needed

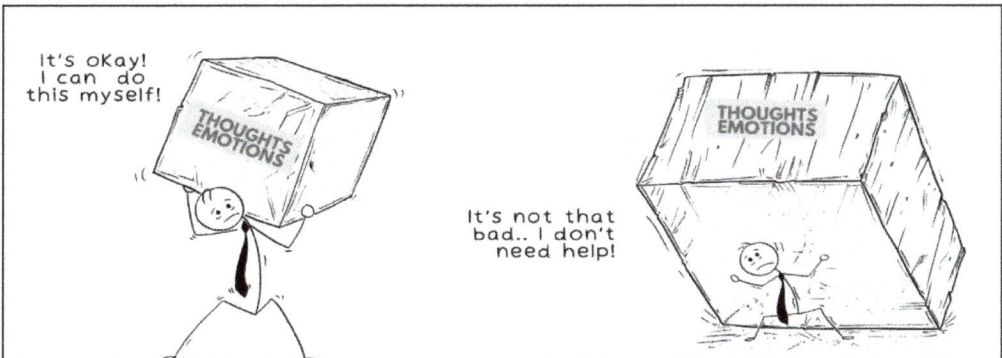

It's common to ignore our mental health until it feels like a crash! But, mental health isn't a 'wait-until-it's-bad' situation, it's more like a car flashing its 'check engine' light—ignore it, and you're risking a breakdown.

Why do we miss the signs?

- We don't always know what signs and symptoms to look for.
- We've gotten used to thinking stress is "normal."
- Not needing help is idolised in hustle culture.
- Symptoms creep in gradually, so we just adapt without noticing the damage.

Even when we know something's off, asking for help can feel like admitting defeat. We worry about being judged, looking weak, or burdening others. Thoughts like "I should be able to handle this," or "No one else can understand" and emotions of guilt & shame can stop us from reaching out.

But asking for help isn't weakness—it's preventative maintenance. Just like you'd get your car serviced to prevent it from breaking down, seeking mental health support keeps your mind running smoothly.

Here's what mental health support looks like:

1. Social Support:
Leaning on friends, family, & community for advice & comfort

2. Professional Support:
Seeking help from trained psychologist, therapists, psychiatrists to help navigate our thoughts, feelings, and behaviors.

My Safety Squad

My safety squad: Identify & name the people in your life who provide support in various environments. Make sure to mention individuals who may be - Friends, Family, Community, Professionals and Other Contacts.

Friends

Family

Community

Professionals and Other Contacts.

Ignoring mental health doesn't make the struggle go away; it just makes it grow silently. Don't wait for the breakdown—call for a tune-up when things feel "off."

When you're ready to reach out for support, we at Manahsparsh are always here to listen and guide you through. Whether it's a tough day or you just need a bit of clarity, our therapists are **just a message away!**

Reach us at **+91 8956261333**   **manahsparsh@gmail.com**

Tackle Procrastination

Ever found yourself scrolling away on instagram, even though you've got a deadline? Or suddenly deciding that today is the day to organize your closet instead of finishing that report?

Welcome to the wonderful world of procrastination—where we delay what matters in favor of... anything else.

Procrastination is like hitting the snooze button on your responsibilities that can range from minor chores like taking out trash, important decisions like breaking up with your girlfriend or even major responsibilities like doing your taxes! Sure, it feels good in the moment, but it comes with long-term costs:

- Emotional distress (Anxiety, guilt, shame, anger)
- Stress impacting your well-being
- Missed deadlines and performance dips
- Erosion of confidence, self-image, and relationships
- Stunting your personal and professional growth

"Procrastination is the thief of time."
— Edward Young

Most of us who want to give up procrastinating find it really hard!
So, Why is procrastination so sticky? Because, it is natural! Here are some common culprits behind it:

Lack of Motivation
Difficulty starting task (not interesting or rewarding)

Task Difficulty
Intimidated by tasks complex, difficult, cumbersome tasks

Fear of Failure
Avoiding not meeting one's own or others' expectations

Lack of Skills
Lack of planning skills or skills required to do the task

Perfectionism
Need to do it well, perfectly or correctly

Mental Health
Conditions affecting brains executive functioning

Identify the cause of your procrastination

Write down instances when you procrastinated & identify the reason for your it-
1. Lack motivation 2. Fear of Failure 3. Perfectionsim 4. Difficult Task 5. Lack skills

When	Task I procrastinated	My Reason
Mon	Job Applications	Lack of motivation
Tues	Cleaning my room	Task Difficulty & Lack of Motivation

Procrastination BINGO

Mark the techniques that you have tried and those that have worked! Following are the 15 techniques to help you break procrastination.

Prioritise one task do nothing else until this is over	**Resign from distractions** List them down & keep them away	**Offer a Reward** upon completion E.g. IG time, going out etc	**Count the Benefits** & recognize the worth in your pains
Remember the Costs of not doing the task in the long run	**Ask for support:** Delegation Body Doubling Seeking help	**Schedule Start Time:** Alarm for 30 mins prior to starting it	**Take small steps:** Break task down into baby steps & avoid anxiety
Identify your causes Use Exercise in A-Z workbook & know why you procrastinate	**Note past success**: Remind of times you overcame avoidance	**Ask yourself:** Is it humanly possible to do the task with current conditions?	**Try challenging yourself** to do it only for 5 mins. & repeat several times
Identify & challenge your excuses: Give argument that falsifies excuse	**Overcome perfectionism & Anxiety:** Try other linked self-help resources	**Navigate through hurdles** in therapy in case nothing helps	

Uncover Your Patterns

Ever made a plan with friends and thought, "This is going to be so fun!" and then found yourself smiling in excitement?
So, which came first:

The action of smiling | The thought "It'll be fun" | The emotion of excitement

This may seem like a simple question, but understanding the sequence can unlock the blueprint of your behavior.

Why does it matter? Because our thoughts, emotions, and behaviours are connected! By recognizing these patterns, you can predict your reactions and even change them!

But what if we aren't aware of our patterns? We end up getting stuck in the same cycles of stress and discomfort over and over again.

 Imagine two kids A & B playing at the beach. A huge wave is approaching them. 'A' runs away shouting, while 'B' jumps and claps!

Are they in the same situation? Yes. But are they feeling the same emotions? No? Why not? The answer lies in their THOUGHTS!

This highlights how our thoughts cause our emotions which in turn influence our actions.

Let's break it down.

A: Looks at the wave: → thinks "I will get hurt" → feels scared → runs away

B: Looks at the wave: → thinks "Wow! Water" → feels excited → jump & claps

> "People and things do not upset us. Rather, we upset ourselves by believing that they can upset us."
>
> –Albert Ellis

Thought Diary

Maintain the following record for every time you experience a strong emotion. Identify the situation, thought, emotion & reaction. Reflect on how it is not the situation rather your thoughts that lead to your emotions & reactions.

Situation	Thought	Feeling	Reaction
Friend said my new haircut looks great	Yey!	Happy	Smiled and said thank you. Felt confident
Got hit by a car	WTF!! Such a jerk! How can he do this?	Angry	Yelled and abused

Tip You can do this activity to track the thought patterns leading to a specific type of emotion (e.g. anger or anxiety) or reaction (procrastination or crying) as well. For that, do this every time you feel that specific emotion or reaction.

100 People Exercise

Take a situation that caused you distress and imagine 100 different people in that same situation. Write down various thoughts, emotions or reactions that they may have. This exercise helps you see that your response is just one of many possibilities.

Value everything that have Helped You

Ever wonder how you got to where you are today? Was it sheer luck, hard work, or a mix of everything?

Truth is, it's always a combination of 3 factors:

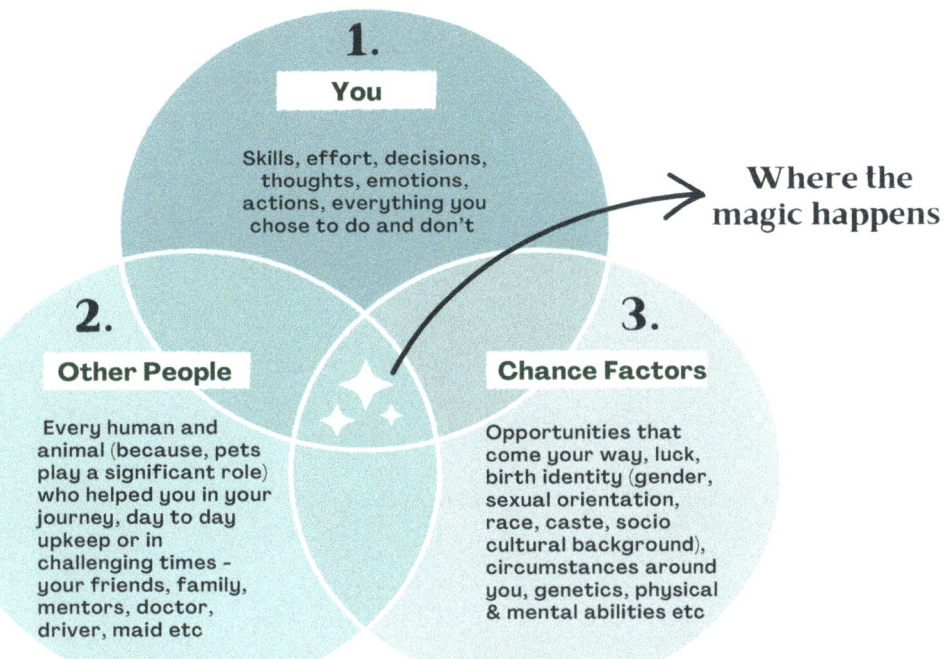

Recognizing & appreciating all the factors—your own actions, the support of others, and the randomness of life—is the essence of gratitude! Success isn't just a one-person show. Without acknowledging what has helped, you can't replicate it. When you're aware of these contributing factors, you can harness them more effectively and cultivate a deeper sense of appreciation for everything valuable—including yourself!

Gratitude not only boosts your well-being but also empowers you to build on your successes:

- Increases awareness of your strengths and resources.
- Helps you replicate successful behaviors and decisions.
- Fosters a positive mindset, enhancing mental well-being.
- Strengthens your connections with others by acknowledging their support.

The Contributors

Note down the role that you, others, chance factors have played in your recent good moment.

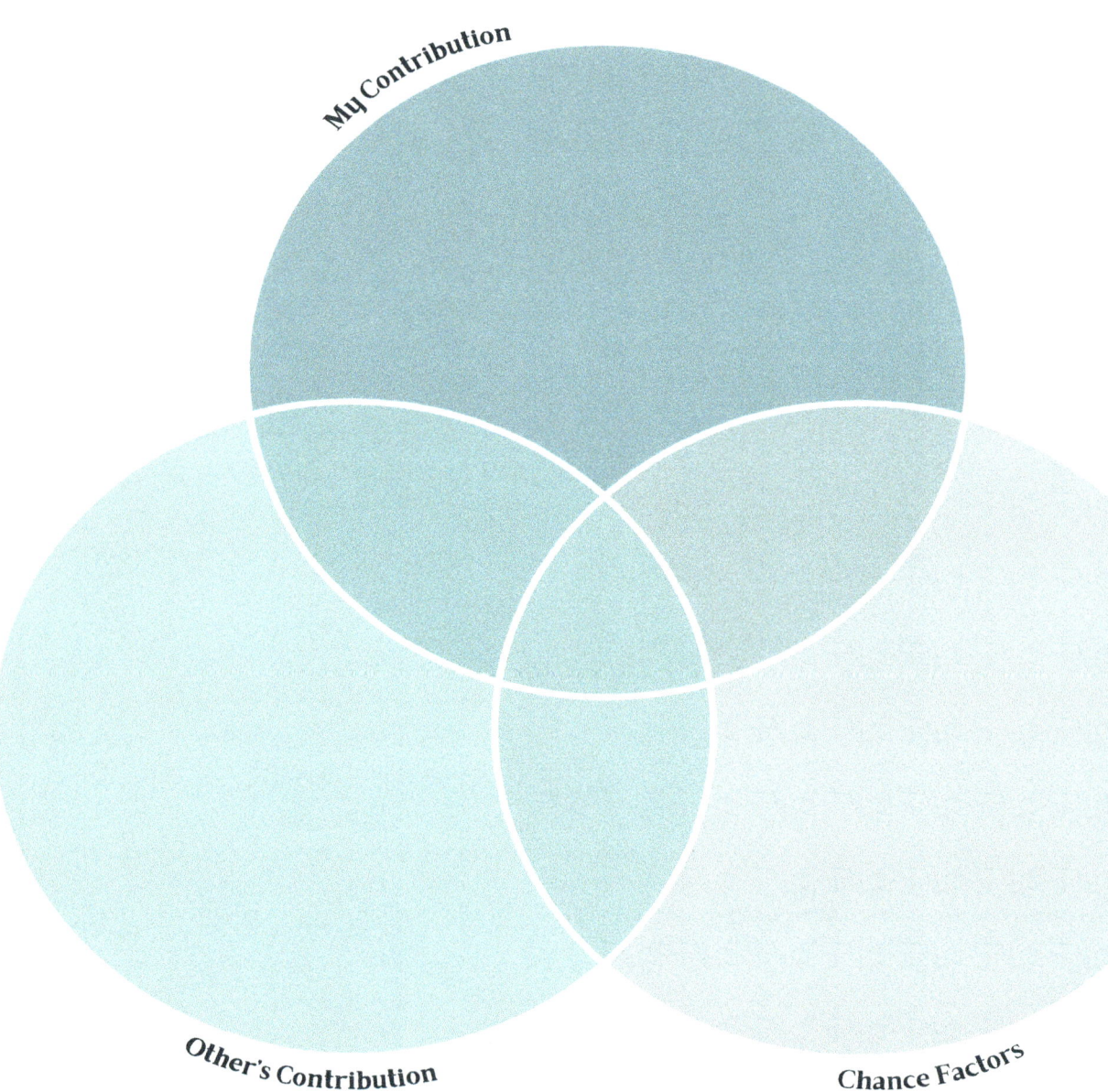

Gratitude Entries

Write entries (daily, weekly or monthly) focusing on things you're grateful for that contributed to your well-being or achievements. Reflect on how you can nurture and sustain these elements in your life.

Work on Your Body

Did you know that a healthier body can lead to a healthier mind?

Our mind & body are inseparable and both affect each other significantly! Understanding the mind-body connection is a powerful tool in maintaining health & wellbeing.

Physical health & wellbeing is the basis of mental health & wellbeing! It impacts your mental state in ways you might not realise. For instance, hormonal imbalances may cause emotional distress while vitamin deficiencies may lead to depressiveness! Even minor pains can significantly affect your mood & behaviour!

Physical Activity	Moderate physical movement is maintains functionality & immunity
Nutrition	Balanced nutrition provides the body with the fuel it needs to perform
Sleep	Adequate quality sleep is essential for rest & recovery

Research shows...

- Regular physical activity can reduce symptoms of depression and anxiety by releasing endorphins—your brain's natural feel-good chemicals

- Hormonal imbalances, such as low thyroid hormones or cortisol spikes, can lead to emotional distress

- Vitamin deficiencies—like B12 or vitamin D—are linked to depressive symptoms

- Minor physical discomforts, like chronic pain or fatigue, can also have an outsized impact on your mood and behavior.

- Untreated chronic pain often leads to anxiety and depression.

By focusing on your physical health, you're not only enhancing your body but also building a stronger, more resilient mind. You'll experience improved mood, better sleep, and a heightened sense of well-being

Maintaining Physical Health

 ## Exercise

Helps maintain physical activity. Floods your brain with endorphins (feel-good chemicals). Incorporate aerobic activities to get heart rate up (130+ bpm) at least 20 minutes a day, target to exercise 3 hours per week and focus on flexibility, stamina & strength

 ## Sleep

Vital for growth, healing, and effective mental functioning. Body's most natural form of rest. Get 7-8 hours of sleep every day with at least 5 hours sun-down sleep. Follow sleep hygiene & a consistent sleep routine for uninterrupted, restful sleep.

 ## Nature Time

Exposure to sunlight and fresh air can elevate your mood and clear your mind. Spend at least 20-30 minutes outside each day, ideally in natural surroundings. Whether it's a walk in the park, gardening, or simply sitting in the sun, make nature time a daily habit.

 ## Caring for Your Body

Personal hygiene and addressing physical issues promptly can prevent mental stress and anxiety. Maintain regular hygiene practices, promptly address physical pains or symptoms; & follow prescribed treatments.

 ## Healthy Diet

A balanced diet provides the necessary nutrition to fuel your body and mind. Eat three balanced meals a day, focusing on whole grains, lean proteins, fruits, & vegetables. Avoid processed foods, excessive sugar, & high-fat items. Drink 2.5-3 litres of water throughout the day.

 ## Avoiding Substance Abuse

Substance abuse can severely impact both physical and mental health. Avoid frequent & excessive use of alcohol, tobacco, drugs, & other harmful substances. Seek professional help if you are struggling with substance use.

Healthy Habit Tracker

Write the habits that you wish to develop and track them for a month to see how you are progressing.

Take care of your body; it's the only place you have to live.

Exercise:

Sleep

Nature time + Sun

Caring for your body

Healthy Diet

Avoiding Substance Abuse

eXpress Yourself Assertively

Let's start with a simple question: Have you ever left a conversation feeling frustrated, either because you didn't say what you meant, or because you said it too harshly? If you're thinking "yes" it is a sign for you to improve your communication style!

Communication involves the expression of thoughts (ideas, opinions), feelings (positive & negative) and needs (desires, expectations).

There are 3 major communication styles

PASSIVE/SUBMISSIVE	ASSERTIVE	AGGRESSIVE/DOMINATING
Holding back from communicating directly & honestly	The ability to communicate directly, honestly, and respectfully without hurting others	One-sided, angry communication without consideration of others
Greater consideration for other than self	Consideration for own as well as other	Greater consideration for self than other
Not Effective: Self sabotaging, People pleasing, 100% chance of hurting self (I definitely lose while they win)	Most Effective: Healthy, helpful, greatest chance of resolution & success, 50% chance that others get hurt (Great chance that both win)	Not Effective: Blaming, condescending, Intimidating, Yelling 100% chance of hurting other (They definitely lose while I win)
Involves agreeing quickly, anxiety, avoidance, hesitation, nervousness, over-apologizing, avoid eye contact, soft voice, fidgeting, not making decision, refusing compliments	Involves negotiation, request, understanding, empathy, appreciation, honesty, respectful language, confident but pleasant tone, maintaining eye contact	Blaming, rude language, condescending tone, belittling & ridiculing, intimidating, threatening, raising voice, yelling, insulting, threatening, physical/verbal abuse, bullying,

PASSIVE/SUBMISSIVE	ASSERTIVE	AGGRESSIVE/DOMINATING
- Frustration of always losing	+ Able to take a stand for self & others	- Disrespectful, abusive, intimidating
- Regret not saying something	+ Say "No" to requests & persuasion	- Unfair
- Hurt, anger, resentment	+ Draw boundaries	- Leads to dislike & hostility
- Dissatisfaction in relationship	+ Have confrontations	- Escalates argument
- Imbalanced, unequal, unfair relationship	+Provide constructive criticism	- Loss of trust in relationship
- Feel disrespected & taken for granted	+ Maintaining relationships	- Triggers anxiety, avoidance, fear, defensiveness in others
- Frustration may piles up & leads to outbursts	+ Effective conflict management	- Leads to dislike & in genuine relationships

My Communication Styles

Identify your communication patterns by writing down 2 situations where you were Assertive, 2 situations where you were Passive, 2 situations where you were Passive-Aggressive, and 2 situations where you were Aggressive.

Passive/Submissive

Passive/Aggressive

Aggressive

Sandwich Model

Communicating assertively can be challenging, but it's a skill you can develop. The sandwich model is one of the most effective techniques for assertive communication. It allows you to convey your message tactfully while maintaining a respectful and supportive atmosphere. It involves three key components

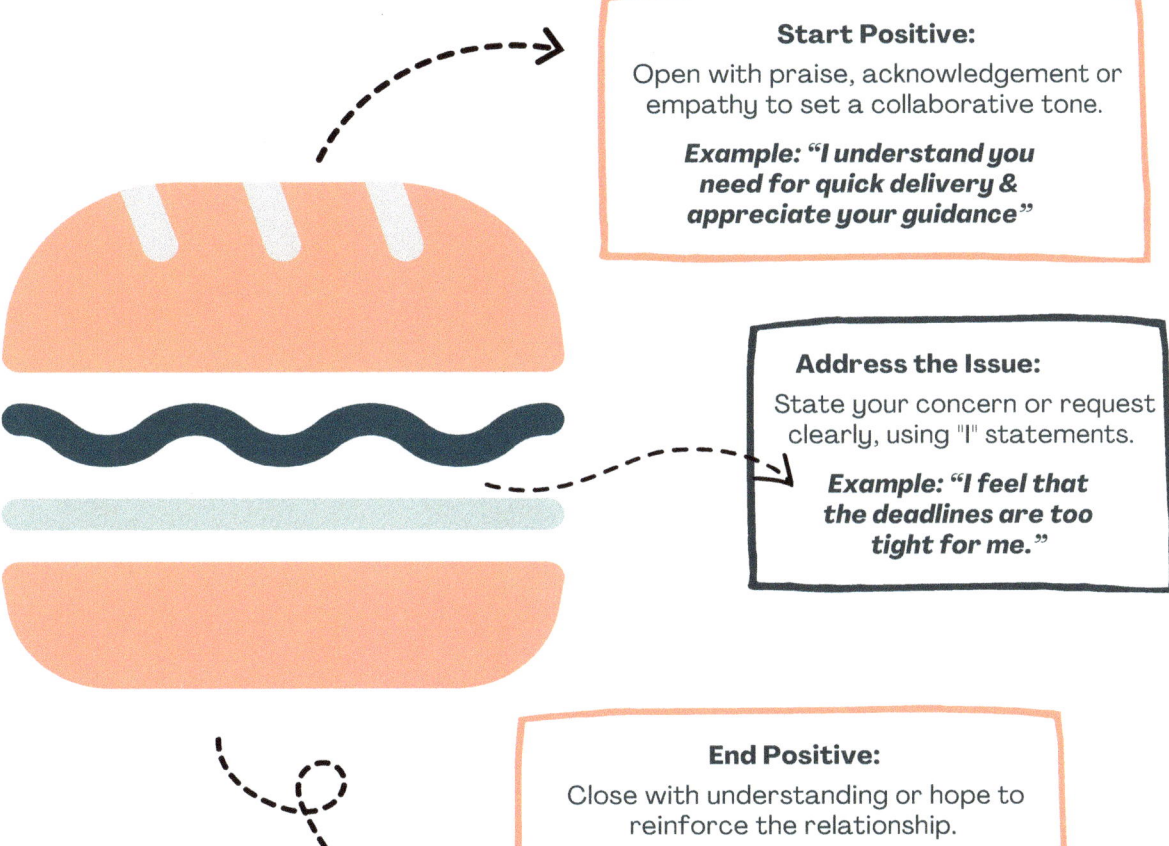

Start Positive:

Open with praise, acknowledgement or empathy to set a collaborative tone.

Example: "I understand you need for quick delivery & appreciate your guidance"

Address the Issue:

State your concern or request clearly, using "I" statements.

Example: "I feel that the deadlines are too tight for me."

End Positive:

Close with understanding or hope to reinforce the relationship.

Example: "I'm confident that with more time, we can deliver even better results"

Tips

Tips: Be honest & precise | avoid generalizing ("always", "never") | Do not blame | Keep it short and collaborative | Use "I" instead of "You" | Focus on solution not the problem

Assertive communication

After completing the first challenge, take situations from above where you communicated in a non-assertive manner and write how you could've reacted assertively using the sandwich method.

How I Commnicated

PASSIVE/SUBMISSIVE

I couldn't say no to my colleague when he called me at 10 pm to ask for some work related help.

AGGRESSIVE/ DOMINATING

I yelled at my mother when she repeatedly asked me to do some chores while I was working on something important.

PASSIVE/ AGGRESSIVE

I was upset with my friend because she made plans with her other friends instead of going out with me so I didn't answer her calls.

How I Could've Communicated

I would like to help you out with this however, I'm off of work right now. Could you call me tomorrow during my working hours and I can help you out then. Thanks for always understanding.

I wish I could help you out with the chores right now, but I am currently busy with office work. Can I help you out once I'm done with this and then we could both sit and watch something nice on the tv.

I was very excited to go out with you and I didn't like that you ditched our plans, let's make sure this doesn't happen next time.

How I Commnicated

PASSIVE/SUBMISSIVE

AGGRESSIVE/ DOMINATING

PASSIVE/ AGGRESSIVE

How I Could've Communicated

Yearn to Set and Achieve Your Goals

Have you also set a goal that felt motivating & exciting, only to abandon it halfway up?

Don't beat yourself, we all have skeletons of abandoned goals in our closet!

Think of goals like the clothes in your cupboard—not all of them are equal, but each plays a role. Some are everyday essentials, like your trusty blue jeans—these are the long-term goals that anchor your life. But just as you can't live your whole life in blue jeans, you need other goals too—those that suit the wedding season, the vacation vibes, or that quirky theme party.

Some goals evolve over time, just like fashion, while others come with baggage you can't quite let go of. It's okay to have goals you outgrow or only use once. Not everything needs to be permanent or fully utilised. And just like clothes that take up space without adding value- like the old-fashioned shirt your dad gifted you, the trendy hat you borrowed from a friend or the really expensive jacket you bought last year - it's okay to let go of goals that no longer serve you.

> **Your capacity, like your cupboard, is limited. Make space for what really matters!**

Here's cycle of steps that will help you to set & achieve your goals consistently:

1. Make space for desirable goals:
Withdraw emotionally and mentally from goals that make you unhappy or aren't yours. Focus your time, energy, and resources on goals that align with your values and bring meaning.

2. Set SMART Goals
That are specific, measurable, achievable, relevant & time bound E.g. Instead of "I want to take a road trip" set a goal to "I want take a Mumbai-Delhi-Mumbai road trip with my partner from 20th Dec to Jan 2nd"

3. Plan your goals:
Break goals into smaller, manageable steps and keep the plan flexible for adjustments. Ensure each step is SMART.

4. Start:
Take that first step, no matter how small. Do not wait for ideal conditions or Monday! Make an imperfect start.

5. Sustain:
Keep moving forward. Focus on progress rather than outcome in spite of failures, or inconsistencies. Such delays are commas, not full stops! Adjust the plan if required.

6. Make it smartER:
Evaluate & Review—don't be afraid to revise or even scrap goals that no longer serve you.

SMART Goals

Set SMART Goals by answering the following questions in the next page

S — **SPECIFIC**
- What is it that I want to accomplish?
- Why is this goal important to me?
- Who are the stakeholders involved in this?
- Where is this goal going to be achieved?
- Which resources will I use here?
- When do I want to achieve this goal?

M — **MEASURABLE**
- How many/much?
- How do I know when I have reached my goal?
- What are the indicators based on which I will know if I have reached my goals?
- How will I measure my progress?

A — **ACHIEVABLE**
- How do I accomplish this goal?
- Is my goal realistic given my current situation - health, resources, time, other commitments & responsibilities?
- Do I have enough resources to make it happen?

R — **RELEVANT**
- Is this goal worthwhile for me?
- Am I in the right place to achieve this?
- Does this goal align well with my other goals?
- Am I the right person to pursue this goal?
- Does this goal apply to the current scenario?
- Am I willing to do what this goal requires?

T — **TIME BOUND**
- When do I accomplish this task?
- Where do I see myself halfway down the line?
- What should be the kind of progress that I display?
- Which daily tasks do I need to do to make sure I achieve my goal on time?
- What are the deadlines for different milestones?

S
SPECIFIC

M
MEASURABLE

A
ACHIEVABLE

R
RELEVANT

T
TIME BOUND

Your Goals at a Glance

Use this activity annually to set and track long-term goals in key areas like mental health, physical health, career, relationships, finances, and lifestyle. Write your SMART goals for each category in the space below to stay focused and aligned with your growth.

Financial	Health & Wellbeing
☐ ☐ ☐ ☐ ☐ ☐ ☐	☐ ☐ ☐ ☐ ☐ ☐ ☐
☐ ☐ ☐ ☐ ☐ ☐ ☐	☐ ☐ ☐ ☐ ☐ ☐ ☐
☐ ☐ ☐ ☐ ☐ ☐ ☐	☐ ☐ ☐ ☐ ☐ ☐ ☐

Zero Down on the Controllable

Are you spiralling with thoughts like the above...

When life throws us curveballs, it's easy to get stuck in a loop of overthinking. In such times, we may find ourselves worrying and/or ruminating about things that are out of our control - like others' opinions & actions or future uncertainties.

But, is thinking about what I can't change or control helping you in any way?   YES / NO

> It only leads to more stress and frustration!
> Instead, the key is to shift your focus to what you can control—your actions, responses, and mindset. It's like adjusting your mental GPS from the problem zone to the solution zone, steering you towards peace and productivity.

By zeroing in on what you can control, you reduce unnecessary stress and increase your ability to act effectively. It helps you stay grounded, improves decision-making, and empowers you to respond rather than react.

This shift not only improves your mental well-being but also boosts your sense of agency and confidence.

> *"It's not what happens to you, but how you react to it that matters."*
> – Epictetus

When you find yourself spiraling out of control, overwhelmed by a flood of thoughts—especially negative ones—it's often because your mind is hijacking your ability to think clearly or take action. In these moments, it's crucial to reconnect with reality and ground yourself in the present. The goal is to break free from unproductive, unhealthy thinking patterns and regain a sense of control.

Break Overthinking

Two powerful techniques that can help you do this are STOPP and the 5-4-3-2-1 Sensory Grounding method. These tools are designed to bring you back to the present moment, helping you to disconnect from overwhelming thoughts and regain clarity.

S — Say "STOP" when you catch yourself overthinking!

T — Take a deep breath. The breath serves as an anchor for the here and now.

O — Observe your anxiety. Take note of what's going on - both within and outside of you. Where has your mind gone? How are you feeling?

P — Pull back: Do unrelated activity or change your thoughts.

P — Proceed to do the task that you were doing!

Grounding Technique

5 things you can see

4 things you can touch

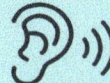

3 things you can hear

2 things you can smell

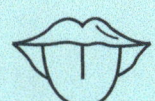

1 thing you can taste

Circle of Control

Write down aspects of the upcoming situation, in the inner circle, write down the factors you can control. In the outer area, list the factors you can't control. Focus your energy on the factors in the inner circle, and set aside the outer factors for later.

Cannot control

Can control

Brain dump

Brain dump

Favourite concepts, ideas

Favourite concepts, ideas

Rational (not positive) Affirmations

Rational (not positive) Affirmations

To use when you are in Distress:

Pg no.	Modules	Exercises
01	A: Accept Yourself	Circle of self | Best have Blemishes
05	B: Be kind to yourself	Replace yourself
15	E: Evaluate Long Term	Cost Benefit Analysis
17	F: Focus on Greys	All things Grey | How Grey am I?
25	H: Have realistic Expectations	Expectation vs Outcome | Challenging "shoulds"
28	I: Improve Capacity to Tolerate Shit	Pain is Gain | Endure & Conquer
35	K: Know & tame your stress	Goodbye Stress
38	L: Look at life as a whole	Life's a pie
43	N: Navigate through your emotions	What am I feeling?| Unpacking emotions
47	O: Overcome Fear of Judgement	Me vs What people think
50	P: Practice Self Regulation	Impulse Tracker | Roadmap to self control
53	Q: Question your Thoughts	Sort my thoughts | Fix my thoughts
56	R: Recognize your role in your distress	How I upset myself | How to stop upsetting myself
61	T: Tackle Procrastination	Decoding procrastination | Get things Done Bingo
82	Z: Zero down focus on what you can control	Break overthinking | Circle of control

In case this workbook isn't enough and you continue to feel distressed, consider contacting us.

We are here to help you find the clarity you need!

To use when you focused on Self-awareness and Development:

Pg no.	Modules	Exercises
08	C: Cultivate meaningful Relationships	Strengthening relationships
12	D: Do things that matter	The PLUS Factor | Activities Menu Card
20	G: Get Quality Sleep	My Good Night Ritual | Sleep Tracker
32	J: Jot Down your strengths	My Superpowers
35	K: Know & tame your stress	Goodbye Stress
40	M: Maintain Balanced Lifestyle	Time Detective | Audit your Lifestyle
59	S: Seek help when needed	My Safety Squad | My therapist
64	U: Uncover your patterns	Thought-reaction | One situation, Many reactions
67	V: Value what helped you	The contributors | Gratitude Journal
70	W: Work on your Body	Habit Tracker
73	X: eXpress Assertively	My communication styles | Being Assertive
77	Y: yearn to set & achieve your goals	SMART goals | Goals at a glance

You commitment towards your self is admirable! In case wish to discover and overcome the roadblocks that keep you from being your best self, choose to contact us!

We will be honoured to assist you in your success!

We are here to help you find the clarity you need!

I sincerely hope this self-help guide has been a valuable companion in your journey of self-development. My goal was to create a workbook that truly feels like your personalized toolkit— something you can lean on as you navigate the ups and downs of life. Use this guide as a reminder to prioritize yourself and support your mental well-being, no matter the challenges you face. Your journey is your own, but I always want to be a part of your incredible life, cheering you on from the sidelines. Thank you for choosing me to be a part of it. I hope this toolkit serves you well for many years to come. And who knows? Maybe you've enjoyed having me as a therapist on your shelf just as much as I've enjoyed creating this for you!

Barkha Nayak
Founder, Manahsparsh

Psychologist, Therapist
(And now, author of this book)

www.ingramcontent.com/pod-product-compliance
Lightning Source LLC
LaVergne TN
LVHW070601070526
838199LV00011B/459